American Justice 2018

Garrett Epps, Consulting Editor

American Justice 2018
The Shifting Supreme Court

Todd Ruger

PENN

UNIVERSITY OF PENNSYLVANIA PRESS

PHILADELPHIA

Published by
University of Pennsylvania Press
Philadelphia, Pennsylvania 19104-4112
www.upenn.edu/pennpress

Printed in the United States of America

A Cataloging-in-Publication record is available from the Library of Congress

Cover design by John Hubbard

ISBN 978-0-8122-5085-5

Contents

The End of the Kennedy Court

The most important moment in the U.S. Supreme Court's most recent term came on its final day, June 27, 2018, with the revelation of one of the most closely guarded secrets in American politics.

The clues were all around. Justice Anthony M. Kennedy was about to turn eighty-two years old. His wife, Mary, attended the last oral arguments of the term. His writing in one of the term's final cases sounded notes of resignation that he had done all he could with his time on the court. His grandchildren showed up in the courtroom on the last day of the term to watch the justices announce the court's decisions.

But few knew Kennedy's plans. Some court watchers had connected the dots and speculated that the longest-serving justice was leaving the court. Similar predictions of Kennedy's retirement had proved false a year earlier, but as the Washington, D.C. summer heated up, so again did the rumors. Hadn't Kennedy appeared chummy at public events with President Donald Trump, the man who would pick his successor? Wouldn't Kennedy be concerned about what that choice would mean for his legacy on women's access to abortion and gay rights? Would he really want such a divisive president to name a second Supreme Court justice?

The nine months of the 2017 October Term* had tested the justices on numerous high-profile and controversial social issues: Trump's travel ban that appeared to target Muslims, Christian businesses that turned away gay customers, and even a fight over political districts in which one side contended the very future of the country's representative democracy was at stake. Justice Neil Gorsuch, diving into his first full term, helped deliver a stream of conservative decisions that exposed discord among the justices and fueled criticism that the court continued to favor Republican interests.

But on that last day before the summer break, Kennedy would upend the court and thrust it even further into the political fray.

Kennedy stepped down from the court in a style lawyers might call "de minimis"—a term generally meaning "an insignificant amount." He passed on a chance to make a grand retirement announcement from the bench. Instead, he sent the White House an unadorned two-paragraph letter addressed to "My dear Mr. President." He directed the Supreme Court's press office to send out a news release with only one quote from him: "It has been the greatest privilege to serve our nation in the federal judiciary for

---

* The Supreme Court convenes, by law, on the first Monday of October. This begins what is known as a new "October Term," with the year of that October covering all the cases heard and decided between then and the end of the following June.

43 years, 30 of those years on the Supreme Court." He met with news reporters who cover the Supreme Court—but only if they agreed not to publish anything he said.

The fallout for the Supreme Court and the nation, however, is anything but de minimis. Kennedy spent the previous decade as the deciding vote in the court's most contentious cases—those dealing with the country's most polarizing political and social issues. Over the years, he had backed access to abortion, led the way on gay rights, and cut down campaign finance laws. In many cases, the nine-member court would split ideologically between four reliably liberal justices and four typically conservative justices. That left Kennedy as a so-called swing vote who could join either side. Usually, he sided with the conservative wing, but sometimes he joined the liberals.

That spot in the middle meant Kennedy's views played an outsized role in shaping the court, and by extension, he held great sway over how the nation's court system altered the cultural and political landscape. Entire cases were constructed around winning him over. His words during oral arguments were analyzed, and overanalyzed. That was particularly true during the 2017 October Term in cases about LGBT rights, the future of online commerce, and the drawing of political maps. It might have been hard to predict his retirement, but it was easy for court watchers to foresee his departure as a momentous change for the institution and the nation.

"This Supreme Court vacancy is among the most consequential of my lifetime," Delaware Democrat Senator Chris Coons, a member of the Senate Judiciary Committee, told reporters. "In just the past few weeks, as the Supreme Court has issued decisions on voting rights, taxes, privacy, labor rights, executive power, and police searches, we've seen as clearly as ever that our courts matter in the lives of every American."

Those decisions served not just as the final word on major legal issues but as a window into the balance of power within the court itself—one upended by Kennedy's announcement on the final day. The cases revealed how major issues arrive at the court, how the justices view the role of the court in shaping American society, and how much politics in turn shapes what happens in the courtroom.

But the 2017 October Term will be remembered as Kennedy's last.

The vacancy Kennedy left behind threw the Supreme Court headfirst into the political fray at an overheated moment in American history. Trump would get to name Kennedy's successor, ensuring that this person would be reliably conservative. The effort to confirm that pick would thrust the Senate into a high-pitched battle at a time when Republicans and Democrats in Washington, D.C. were already in an all-out war over just about every other aspect of political life.

Throughout the court's 2017 October Term, Trump proved to be an unpredictable president who charted a far different course in decorum and statecraft than his predecessors. He displayed a loose relationship with the truth and the details of governmental policies, and he often attacked the legal system and the judges in it. A special counsel investigation dug into connections between his campaign and Russian operatives who interfered in the presidential election that delivered Trump to the presidency. His immigration policies drew protests. The divide was cultural as well: even title-winning professional sports teams didn't make traditional visits to the White House amid objections from players and coaches about the president's racially tinged rhetoric and policies.

At the same time, a hyperpartisan Congress, controlled by the Republicans and in a near constant state of gridlock, appeared unable or unwilling to respond to Trump and his passionate base of supporters. George F. Will, a longtime conservative columnist, described it all as "a carnage of Republican misrule in Washington" and urged the country to vote for Democrats in the November 2018 elections. Democrats escalated their opposition to almost anything Trump did. A middle ground among everyday Americans appeared to be rapidly disappearing, fueled by cultural divisions and an exhausting around-the-clock news cycle that featured an endless series of scandals and crises.

Trump's Supreme Court pick would have to navigate through this partisan obstacle course. With Republicans controlling the Senate, conservatives anticipated replacing the justice in the center with a justice well to his right. It would tip the court's ideological center of gravity in a conservative direction. Democrats and their allies were apoplectic, warning that any Trump pick would erase Kennedy's middle-ground positions, that abortion rights in the country were doomed, and that progress for LGBT rights was set for reversal.

Within weeks, advocacy groups on both sides had spent millions of dollars in television and Internet advertising campaigns to either back or attack the nominee— even before they knew who it was. The confirmation showdown promised to play out in several days of televised hearings just ahead of the 2018 midterm elections.

There would no doubt be senators criticizing the court's decisions as political and trying to cast the nominee as a partisan ideologue.

In a floor speech the day Trump was set to announce his choice to succeed Kennedy, Majority Leader Mitch McConnell, R-Ky., commented about how one Democratic senator had already predicted that Trump's pick would bring about the destruction of the Constitution. "It is hard to keep a straight face when you hear stuff like that," McConnell said. "There is not even a nominee yet."

The Supreme Court would rather not be in this kind of political hot seat. The justices, apart from a book tour or rare guest appearance on a late-night talk show, keep a low public profile. They conduct much of their business the way Kennedy announced his retirement—behind closed doors, outside of the view of cameras, and in a controlled setting. As an institution, the Supreme Court is a close guardian of information, even in the least controversial of times. It historically acts cautiously, tries to cultivate a perception that it operates above politics, and insists that the justices are not politically motivated.

The court's proceedings are not televised. The justices say they don't want oral arguments turned into a contest to see who can get a soundbite on the evening news. They strive to reach consensus among themselves and strive to persuade the greatest possible number of justices to join the majority in each decision, so that the court will come close to speaking with one voice. The Supreme Court's power and legitimacy are tied to its institutional reputation—and to whether the public views its decisions as fair and apolitical. The court was at its least popular in

2015, the Pew Research Center found, when Republicans objected to major decisions announcing a constitutional right to same-sex marriage and upholding the Affordable Care Act for the second time.

But the court has been unwittingly awash in politics since February 2016, with the death of conservative Justice Antonin Scalia. Democratic President Barack Obama had an opportunity to appoint a justice, but McConnell, a Republican who puts great emphasis on elevating conservatives to the federal courts, immediately announced that the Senate would not confirm any nominee until after the 2016 presidential election. Obama's pick, Merrick Garland, stalled in the Senate. Trump won the election and appointed Gorsuch. McConnell then changed long-standing Senate rules so that Democrats, who were in the minority, could not block a confirmation vote, and Gorsuch took the bench in April 2017.

Democrats haven't forgotten, and the wounds are still fresh. They still consider Gorsuch to be occupying a stolen seat on the court, and they use this conviction to attack the authority of the court's rulings. As California Senator Dianne Feinstein, the Judiciary Committee's top Democrat, put it after a ruling that backed a Trump policy just before the end of the 2017 October Term: "Today's decision is yet another reminder of the importance of our courts and the grave injustice of Leader McConnell's decision to block the appointment of Merrick Garland."

Even before he was confirmed, Gorsuch aimed to defend the Supreme Court's reputation against such attacks. At his Senate confirmation hearing in 2017, the gray-haired Coloradoan told senators that the plain black robes the justices wear are a reminder of the "modest station" that judges occupy in the U.S. democracy, with its three branches of government. "These days we sometimes hear judges cynically described as politicians in robes, seeking to enforce their own politics rather than striving to apply the law impartially. If I thought that were true, I'd hang up the robe," Gorsuch said. "But I just don't think that's what a life in the law is about."

In some important ways, Gorsuch's explanation of "judicial restraint" simply defines the role of the Supreme Court in the American system. The justices can't write laws; that's up to Congress. They can't enforce the laws; that's up to the president. They can only agree to hear the cases that are brought before them. When the court issues an opinion, it publicly recounts its legal reasoning for doing so. And even then, the justices are constrained by the presumption that they will adhere to such legal principles as *stare decisis,* which holds that a court should stick to its previous decisions unless there are good reasons for abandoning them.

Chief Justice John G. Roberts Jr. famously described this idea during his 2005 confirmation hearing by comparing judges to baseball umpires simply "calling balls and strikes." In the real world, though, the business of the court is not so straightforward. If it were, a Supreme Court impartially applying the law to the facts in a case would rule 9–0 every time. Many Supreme Court decisions are unanimous. But it is generally only the most tangled cases that make it to the Supreme Court—often those in which the answer is so unsettled that judges in lower courts have split on how to rule.

When the nine justices of the Supreme Court vigorously disagree with one another, the country gets the best glimpse of their conflicting views on how to interpret laws and the Constitution, and of their various philosophies about the role of the court in American government. The deliberations are done in private. Unlike what happens in the White House and Congress, leaks from the Supreme Court to the media are virtually unheard of. But in the opinions, each side explains why they are right and the other side is wrong. There were plenty of those split decisions in the 2017 October Term.

Five of the justices decided that a law about immigrants should be struck down as unconstitutional, and four disagreed. Five justices ruled that there was a good reason to reverse an old Supreme Court ruling on union fees, and four thought they had it wrong. Five justices pressed for the Supreme Court to step in and issue a sweeping ruling affecting a large sector of the economy, and four thought the court went too far. Five decided that the Supreme Court shouldn't rein in a president when it comes to national security and the nation's borders, and four thought the court shirked its responsibility.

In all these cases, the justices looked at the same facts, the same laws, the same precedents, and came to differing conclusions about what the court should do.

During the 2017 October Term, there were eighteen cases in which the court split 5–4 (and one that came down 5–3). In most of them, the court divided along ideological lines that reflect the political party of the president who appointed them. That meant Chief Justice Roberts and Justices Clarence Thomas, Kennedy, Samuel A. Alito Jr., and Gorsuch, all appointed by Republican presidents, came down on one side, while Justices Ruth Bader

Ginsburg, Stephen G. Breyer, Sonia Sotomayor, and Elena Kagan, appointed by Democratic presidents, came down on the other.

Kennedy's penchant for crossing that ideological divide explains why he played such a pivotal role in the outcome of cases, and what makes his legacy so mixed from the perspectives of both the political left and right. He was hard to predict and ended up serving as a moderating force. But his departure also underscores why politicians see the confirmation fight over Kennedy's seat as so important, and why it threatens to erode public confidence in the court.

As the chief justice, Roberts has largely taken on the role of guardian of the Supreme Court's reputation. He described his view of the role of the court in his dissent in *Obergefell v. Hodges,* the 5–4 decision that established a constitutional right to same-sex marriage in 2015. In that case he disagreed with the outcome and criticized the court for overturning the marriage laws of more than half the states in the country. He saw the decision as a group of unelected justices changing the nature of a social institution that had formed the basis of human society for millennia. "Just who do we think we are?" Roberts wrote.

Respect for the court's decisions, he wrote, "flows from the perception—and reality—that we exercise humility and restraint in deciding cases according to the Constitution and law." The legitimacy of the court ultimately rests on the respect given its judgments, and the court majority in *Obergefell* moved too far and too fast on the issue that voters in states were still deciding, he wrote. "Five lawyers have closed the debate and enacted their own vision of marriage as a matter of constitutional law," he wrote of the majority. "Stealing this issue from the people will for many cast a cloud over same-sex marriage, making a dramatic social change that much more difficult to accept."

The main target of his criticism was Kennedy, who wrote the majority opinion in *Obergefell*. It was the latest in a series of decisions in which Kennedy had sided with the liberal wing of the court to advance gay rights. That's the power Kennedy enjoyed as the center of the court. He could pick and choose when the court should stay reserved or strike out with a bold ruling that overturns laws or the court's own precedents.

Roberts might have been the chief justice, but it was Kennedy's court. Now, with Kennedy gone, Roberts could become the new center of the court as well as its chief justice, making him all the more powerful in shaping when the court steps in and how boldly it does so.

The 2017 October Term was supposed to be one in which the court would have a full complement of justices and be able to settle back into the routine of its work. The court had been shorthanded for more than fourteen months after Scalia's death, and ideologically split 4–4. The justices largely refrained from considering major cases during that time and ended up deadlocked on some of them. After Gorsuch's confirmation in April 2017, the court filled its docket with consequential and high-profile cases at the heart of some of the nation's biggest social and political fights. "As somebody who watches the court's term very closely, I don't know that I can remember a term with so many big-ticket cases on the court's docket," former Solicitor General Paul Clement told the Republican National Lawyers Association.

Cases on partisan gerrymandering and about a religious baker who declined to make a cake for a same-sex wedding highlight how lawyers targeted Kennedy's vote on sweeping political and social questions. Decisions on Internet sales taxes and cell phone records show how individual justices can sway national policy, affecting either one of the largest sectors of the nation's economy or Americans' privacy in their movements. A ruling on Trump's travel ban revealed the contours of the court's power compared to the president's. Opinions in cases on unions, abortion clinics, and workers' rights demonstrated the conservative bent of the current court.

There was also the looming question of how the court would react to the Trump administration's Justice Department, which exerted its influence in high-profile cases. "I do think the Trump administration has cranked up the heat around the importance of the court standing for the strengthening of democratic principles and pillars that will hold this country together," Sherrilyn Ifill, NAACP Legal Defense and Educational Fund president and director-counsel, said ahead of the term. "It would be surprising to me if they didn't all feel the press of that."

Just before the start of the term, Justice Ginsburg summed up the court's docket in a way that ended up in plenty of news stories. In a speech to a group of Georgetown University Law Center students, she said, "There is only one prediction that is entirely safe about the upcoming term, and that is it will be momentous."

Nobody would dissent from that opinion.

Drawing Political Lines

Gerrymandering is a political tradition as old as America's democracy. Politicians draw the boundaries of political districts within their state, carving out the areas that members of Congress or state legislators represent. So, of course, both Republicans and Democrats manipulate those lines to create an advantage for their political party and their political allies. The term *gerrymandering* emerged from an election in 1812.

But as the Supreme Court convened more than two hundred years later for the 2017 October Term, advocates for fairer elections warned the justices that the abuses of gerrymandering had become so great that they threatened democracy itself. They said that state lawmakers, with the help of increasingly powerful computers and data analytics, could carve maps that would entrench their party in power. Those legislative districts baked in such an advantage that voters were powerless to change which party would win there and represent them in Congress or the statehouse. And that ensured the same party could retain control of drawing the maps—perpetuating a cycle that could leave members of one party entrenched in power, with the other party incapable of dislodging them.

On its face, the case before the justices, *Gill v. Whitford,* was about the ninety-nine statehouse districts in Wisconsin. But the real fight was about whether the Supreme Court would, for the first time, allow federal courts to stop partisan gerrymanders to stem the risk of erosion of the right of Americans to choose their representatives.

And the challengers pressed that the time to act was right now. Republicans and Democrats already had ramped up to spend tens of millions of dollars on efforts to seize control of the redistricting process in key states ahead of the 2020 census. Without the court's intervention, the resulting maps drawn after the census could be so lopsided and enduring that citizens would lose faith that their vote matters, said Paul Smith, an attorney representing voters who challenged Wisconsin's statehouse map.

"We're here telling you, you are the only institution in the United States that can solve this problem, just as democracy is about to get worse, because of the way gerrymandering is getting so much worse," Smith told the justices during oral arguments.

For the "you" in that plea, read in "Justice Anthony M. Kennedy," since the whole issue appeared all but certain to turn on his vote. Kennedy previously had recognized the problems with partisan gerrymandering. But he had struggled with the question of when courts should step in to say there is too much politics in what is always an inherently political process. With his approach to retirement, legal experts predicted this would be his last chance to fix what he considered a major flaw in the American political landscape.

The outcome of the case shows not only how legal groups often targeted Kennedy as the pivotal justice on the most contentious issues of the day, but also how the Supreme Court as an institution, to guard its status and integrity against charges that it favors one party over the other, sometimes treads cautiously into polarizing political disputes.

Through the lens of Kennedy's retirement, the case also provides clues that the court isn't ready to leap into the middle of the high-stakes redistricting battle.

Back in 2004, Kennedy was not shy in criticizing how political the redistricting process had become, in a case called *Vieth v. Jubelirer*. That was the last time the Supreme Court had considered partisan gerrymandering.

Back then, Republicans controlled a majority of Pennsylvania's legislature, as well as the governor's office, and they redrew the state's congressional map after the 2000 Census. It was part of a political scrap. The national Republican Party sought to use the Keystone State's redistricting plan to punish Democrats for partisan gerrymanders in other states. Kennedy was the deciding vote, skewering the behavior, in his characteristically passionate yet restrained style.

"The ordered working of our Republic, and of the democratic process, depends on a sense of decorum and restraint in all branches of government, and in the citizenry itself. Here, one has the sense that legislative restraint was abandoned," Kennedy wrote separately in the case. "That should not be thought to serve the interests of our political order. Nor should it be thought to serve our interest in demonstrating to the world how democracy works."

Yet Kennedy declined to strike down Pennsylvania's map as a partisan gerrymander because of a big question: how do courts determine when politics played too big of a role in creating the district boundaries? Without knowing how to measure that, he wrote, the results from one gerrymandering case to the next would be inconsistent.

There are plenty of ways a political map can be challenged on other grounds—if the lawmakers inappropriately used race to draw lines, for example, or didn't follow standard redistricting principles such as making each district have essentially the same number of people. Plenty of Supreme Court decisions explain how lower courts can decide if a map is unconstitutional. But the partisan gerrymandering standard remained elusive.

Kennedy's position in *Vieth* meant that the Supreme Court at the time would not let courts strike down political maps as partisan gerrymanders. But Kennedy left the door wide open to doing that in the future if his questions were answered.

"If workable standards do emerge to measure these burdens, however, courts should be prepared to order relief," he wrote.

Ten years later, a research fellow's idea appeared to answer Kennedy's call. Eric McGhee at the Public Policy Institute of California came up with a mechanism to express in a single tidy number the systematic advantage a congressional map gives one political party. He worked it into a legal theory with Nicholas Stephanopoulos, then an assistant professor at the University of Chicago Law School, and the duo eventually published a law review article in 2014. They called it the "efficiency gap."

The mechanism uses just a bit of math to boil down the level of partisan gerrymandering in a state. It does so by breaking down how partisan gerrymandering works. State lawmakers who control the redistricting process want their party's candidates to win more seats. One way to help do that is to draw a map that allows their party's candidates to win each district with as few votes to spare as possible, while the opposing party's candidates win in blowouts. That can be achieved in two ways: consolidate the opposing party's voters into a single district, known as packing; or break the opposing party's strongholds in a way that dilutes the votes, known as cracking.

The efficiency gap measures the amount of packing and cracking by counting "wasted votes," or votes that didn't determine the outcome of an election in a district. For example, all votes that Democrats cast in a district where the Democratic candidate loses would be counted as wasted votes. So would votes Democrats cast above the 50 percent level needed in a district where the Democratic candidate wins.

If both parties have the same number of wasted votes across a statewide election, the efficiency gap would be zero. There would be no gap between the wasted votes, so no advantage to one party. If there is a difference, the efficiency gap divides each party's number of wasted votes by the total number of votes in the election, subtracts those two numbers, and the difference is the efficiency gap.

Stephanopoulos, along with the Washington, D.C.–based Campaign Legal Center, used the efficiency gap to pursue a federal lawsuit on behalf of a dozen Democratic Wisconsin voters. The metric showed that the map for state legislative districts that Republican lawmakers enacted in

2011 gave Republicans a big advantage in the 2012, 2014, and 2016 elections. Stephanopoulos described in an opinion piece published in *Vox* that the plaintiffs combined that efficiency gap with other metrics to make a compelling case: the Wisconsin map was more skewed than most historically. That result wasn't because of the geography of the state. And the advantage to Republicans is likely to persist even if the statewide vote swung to Democrats in a historic way.

In 2016, a panel of three federal judges in Wisconsin agreed with the Democratic voters. The court, in a 2–1 vote, struck down the Wisconsin State Assembly's map as a partisan gerrymander—the first time that had happened in more than thirty years. Among the reasons for the ruling, the panel noted the skewed results that can result from skewed lines: Republicans won 61 percent of the state's ninety-nine Assembly seats with just 49 percent of the statewide vote in 2012, and Republicans won 64 percent of the Assembly seats with only 52 percent of the statewide vote in 2014.

Wisconsin officials appealed, and such an elections-related appeal goes directly to the Supreme Court. The justices would have to decide.

The Terminator joined those who urged the Supreme Court to step in to stop partisan gerrymandering.

The actor-turned-California-governor, Arnold Schwarzenegger, who played the killer robot from the future in Hollywood movies, was among a group of Republican former governors and U.S. senators who filed a brief in the case to say that the practice was harming the republican form of government and that politicians refused to fix it on their own.

"Gerrymandering is not a Republican or Democrat issue—it is a voter's issue," Schwarzenegger said when the group's brief was filed at the court. "Politicians of both parties draw maps to benefit their own interests—but never the voters."

Even as Schwarzenegger spoke, the political parties were bulking up and dedicating huge amounts of money for nationwide campaigns to control crucial local offices ahead of the 2020 census. The census requires every state to redraw its congressional maps. Ten years earlier, national party Republicans made a major push to gain those governorships and legislative bodies that would redraw congressional maps after the 2010 census. It largely caught the national Democratic Party flat-footed, and Republicans swept into those positions. The Republican State Leadership Committee already has relaunched its effort for the next census as REDMAP2020, with a goal to raise $125 million to defend those state majorities.

Democrats intend to fight back this time. They say the Republican redistricting advantage allowed Republican candidates to win a thirty-three–seat majority in the House in the 2012 elections, despite winning fewer than half of all votes for Congress. Democrats formed a new group led by former Attorney General Eric H. Holder Jr. and backed by Barack Obama. The group, the National Democratic Redistricting Committee, has targeted twenty legislative chambers, nine gubernatorial races, and other races that it considers the "most important for shifting the balance of power in the redistricting process." It aims to spend $30 million for the 2018 election cycle, including special statehouse races in Minnesota and a Supreme Court race in Wisconsin. The 2018 election is the first election cycle "where the officials elected will serve during the redistricting process in 2021," the group said.

A bipartisan duo of sitting senators, Democrat Sheldon Whitehouse of Rhode Island and the late Republican John McCain of Arizona, warned the justices in a brief that big-money policy influencers used partisan gerrymandering as a tool at the expense of the public and democracy. They blamed the court's *Vieth* decision from 2004 for giving state lawmakers leeway to draw district lines in the zealous pursuit of partisan advantage.

"Americans do not like gerrymandering. They see its mischief, and absent a legal remedy, their sense of powerlessness and discouragement has increased, deepening the crisis of confidence in our democracy," the duo wrote. "From our vantage point, we see wasted votes and silenced voices. We see hidden power. And we see a correctable problem."

The question would be whether Kennedy saw a way for the courts to be the solution.

The rest of the Supreme Court was just as divided as it had been in *Vieth*, even with the Terminator staring back at them from the gallery during oral arguments in one of the first cases in October. The court's four liberals expressed concerns that partisan gerrymandering stacked the deck for a decade and chipped away at the fundamental right to vote by making it meaningless.

The conservative justices cast doubt that the efficiency gap, or any of the other metrics presented to them in the case, gave courts a clear way to resolve partisan gerrymandering claims. Chief Justice John G. Roberts Jr. called them "sociological gobbledygook." Justice Samuel A. Alito Jr. said that gerrymandering was distasteful, but the standard must be manageable and sufficiently concrete. Justice Neil Gorsuch said the lower court's reasoning in using various metrics to conclude that the map is unconstitutional reminded him of his steak rub: "I like some turmeric, I like a few other little ingredients, but I'm not going to tell you how much of each."

But the most telling for the court's future was a long, clearly preplanned description from Roberts about what he said was the "main problem" in the case, with his mind on the court's reputation. Let's call it the "intelligent man on the street" issue:

> I would think if these—if the claim is allowed to proceed, there will naturally be a lot of these claims raised around the country. Politics is a very important driving force and those claims will be raised. And every one of them will come here for a decision on the merits. These cases are not within our discretionary jurisdiction. They're the mandatory jurisdiction.
>
> We will have to decide in every case whether the Democrats win or the Republicans win. So it's going to be a problem here across the board. And if you're the intelligent man on the street and the Court issues a decision, and let's say, okay, the Democrats win, and that person will say: "Well, why did the Democrats win?" And the answer is going to be because EG was greater than 7 percent, where EG is the sigma of party X wasted votes minus the sigma of party Y wasted votes over the sigma of party X votes plus party Y votes.

Chapter 1

And the intelligent man on the street is going to say that's a bunch of baloney. It must be because the Supreme Court preferred the Democrats over the Republicans. And that's going to come out one case after another as these cases are brought in every state. And that is going to cause very serious harm to the status and integrity of the decisions of this Court in the eyes of the country.

If Kennedy knew what he was going to do in the case, he didn't telegraph it. He asked some questions to the lawyer representing Wisconsin about whether the voters in the case had the legal right to bring the case in the first place, called standing. It's a standard threshold issue in a case—should it even be allowed in court?—that routinely comes up and sometimes can be the deciding issue. Later in the argument, Kennedy probed which standard courts should use, whether a partisan gerrymander would be unconstitutional under the First Amendment or the Fourteenth Amendment. It was a repeat of the issue he had grappled with in the *Vieth* case more than a decade earlier.

He didn't ask any questions of Smith, the attorney for the voters.

Months later, the court seemed no closer to a resolution. In December, the Supreme Court agreed to hear arguments in another partisan gerrymandering case, *Benisek v. Lamone*. This time, the gerrymander was a single congressional district in Maryland, which brought different issues and a different legal theory to the court, in part because state officials clearly intended to flip the district from a Republican representative to a Democratic one.

But when the court heard oral arguments on the *Benisek* case in March, the justices appeared just as unsure about where courts might step in.

The court didn't issue a decision for months. When the justices finally did so in the two cases at the end of the term in June, they sidestepped the main issue altogether. Instead of a landmark ruling, the justices joined together in a unanimous compromise, holding that the Wisconsin voters in the *Gill* case had not proven that they had standing. This outcome was reached, as Roberts wrote for the majority, after "considerable effort." The Supreme Court sent the case back to the lower court to give those voters a chance to prove that they deserved to be in court. Justices Thomas and Gorsuch wrote separately in the case only to say they wouldn't have given the voters such a second chance.

Similarly, the court kicked the Maryland case in *Benisek* back to a district court on procedural grounds with little comment and no noted dissents. The courts didn't rule on the main issue in either case, so the nation remains in the same position as it was after the *Vieth* case a decade earlier: the Supreme Court has not yet fully closed the door on the possibility that courts can strike down partisan gerrymanders.

Justice Elena Kagan wrote a concurring opinion in *Gill*, joined by the other three liberal justices, to express the view that courts have a critical role in curbing partisan gerrymandering. She wrote that legislators can entrench themselves in office despite the will of the people, and if the court doesn't step in it would leave citizens without any political remedy for their constitutional harms. The 2010 redistricting cycle produced some of the worst partisan gerrymanders on record, Kagan wrote, and the 2020 cycle will only get worse.

"But of one thing we may unfortunately be sure. Courts—and in particular this Court—will again be called on to redress extreme partisan gerrymanders," Kagan wrote. "I am hopeful we will then step up to our responsibility to vindicate the Constitution against a contrary law."

But that hope seemed to fade with Kennedy's retirement. The court had a chance to step up in the *Gill* case, but it punted. When that case or similar cases come back, they will arrive at a court without Kennedy. Voting rights groups will likely have to hope that Roberts changes his mind about the "intelligent man on the street" criticizing the court's decisions as too political.

Roberts sounded his own note of caution in the majority opinion, when it came to Smith's argument that the Supreme Court is the only institution in the United States capable of solving this problem. "Such invitations must be answered with care," Roberts wrote.

And then Roberts quoted a Kennedy opinion in a 1998 case: "Failure of political will does not justify unconstitutional remedies."

Chapter 2

The Masterpiece Decision

For more than two decades Jack Phillips ran his suburban Denver bakery according to his religious beliefs. The devout Christian chose the name Masterpiece Cakeshop to convey the artistic nature of his custom designs, as well as to refer to his favorite Bible verse, Ephesians 2:10: "For we are God's masterpiece. He has created us anew in Christ Jesus, so we can do the good things He planned for us long ago." He closed the shop on Sundays so he and his employees could attend religious services. His faith convinced him not to design cakes for Halloween, or ones that contain what he considered to be hateful or profane messages, or ones to promote atheism, racism, or indecency.

So when gay couple Charlie Craig and David Mullins went to Masterpiece in the summer of 2012 in their search for a custom cake for their wedding reception, Phillips turned them away. Phillips would later explain that his church teaches marriage is a union between one man and one woman, and it would be against his religious beliefs to lend his baking talents to the celebration of a same-sex marriage.

Craig and Mullins felt humiliated and left the store. And maybe the couple would have simply moved on, if it had been some time in the not-too-distant past, when gays and lesbians were barred from military service, fired from jobs, or targeted by police. That might have been the end of the story, as it was for at least five other same-sex couples that Phillips turned away for the same reason. But the culture in America in 2012 was shifting to greater acceptance of LGBT individuals, and the couple pursued a claim against Phillips under the state's anti-discrimination law.

By the time Craig and Mullins' case made it to the Supreme Court for the 2017 October Term, their Colorado cake fight had become a national one. The case sat at the intersection of two competing major social and legal movements. On one side, civil rights groups have made hard-fought gains for LGBT equality under the law, culminating in a constitutional right to same-sex marriage. And on the other, religiously affiliated groups say these rulings have gone too far and pursued legal cases to fight back in the name of religious rights.

The court needed to decide where to draw the line between anti-discrimination laws and the First Amendment's guarantees of free speech and freedom of religion. Can businesses open generally to the public follow the sincere religious beliefs of their owners and refuse to provide services for LGBT individuals? Can they essentially put up a sign that says, "We do not serve gays"? Or does enforcement of anti-discrimination laws that have long protected racial minorities also apply to sexual orientation, and trump those religious views?

The court's answer has huge implications not only for the nation's cultural landscape but also for the role the

Supreme Court plays in shaping that landscape now and in the future. Colorado isn't the only state facing this type of case, and bakers aren't the only businesses that want to refuse to serve LGBT individuals. A ruling for Craig and Mullins would further solidify LGBT rights. And a ruling for Phillips could unleash a flood of cases that puts the Supreme Court in the business of deciding which companies in which situations have a right to deny services based on the religious views of their owners.

"Hanging in the balance is more than Phillips' freedom to ply his craft without forfeiting his conscience," the baker's attorneys wrote in a brief. "At stake is his and all likeminded believers' freedom to live out their religious identity in the public square. The First Amendment promises them that basic liberty."

The case ultimately showed how the Supreme Court, when faced with a compelling and important social issue, can find a compromise position on a small part of the case that allows them to reach a partial consensus by putting off an ultimate decision on the main issue for another day.

The case also highlights in especially vivid terms just how different the court will be without Justice Anthony M. Kennedy.

There was little doubt that Kennedy would hold the greatest sway over the outcome of the case, *Masterpiece Cakeshop v. Colorado Civil Rights Commission*. As in many other contentious cases, the other justices appeared divided 4–4 along familiar ideological lines. But Kennedy appeared just as divided himself in this case. In his three decades on the bench, he had been a driving force behind wins for LGBT rights, to the chagrin of some religious groups. But he also pressed for tolerance of religious views. At the twilight of his time on the bench, those two legacies were on a collision course, and he was being asked to choose between them.

The Supreme Court first asserted itself on the side of LGBT rights in another case from Colorado in 1996— three years after Phillips opened his bakery. Voters in the Centennial State back then had approved a constitutional amendment to prevent gay and bisexual people from receiving protections under the state's civil rights laws, blocking them from claims of discrimination in workplace, housing, and other areas. In *Romer v. Evans*, the Supreme Court voted 6–3 to strike down that amendment. The state amendment violated the Constitution's Equal Protection Clause because denying these protections didn't advance a legitimate state interest, the court ruled. It was a turnabout from a decade earlier, when the court had last weighed in on gay rights and had upheld a state law that criminalized sodomy. Kennedy wrote the majority opinion in *Romer.*

It was exactly the kind of decision Republicans had worried about when Kennedy had joined the court in 1988. Kennedy hadn't been President Ronald Reagan's first choice to fill the Supreme Court seat. The Senate rejected Reagan's first pick, Robert Bork, after a punishing confirmation process that left both political parties weary. Reagan's second pick, Douglas Ginsburg, took himself out of the running amid reports that he had smoked marijuana. Reagan then turned to Kennedy, a judge on the liberal-leaning U.S. Court of Appeals for the Ninth Circuit based in San Francisco and a more moderate choice.

White House records reveal that the president's advisors worried about Kennedy's past decisions and his views on privacy rights, particularly in a 1980 case, *Beller v.*

Middendorf, in which he "grudgingly" upheld the Navy's regulations prohibiting "homosexual conduct." Kennedy had formulated the rationale in that case much more narrowly than required, the president's advisors wrote in memos now kept at the Reagan presidential library in California. And that could limit the effect of a Supreme Court precedent that Republicans had cheered, the 1986 case that upheld a state's criminalization of homosexual conduct. Kennedy would go on to become the court's voice on gay rights. He wrote the majority opinion in *Lawrence v. Texas,* the 6–3 decision in 2003 that struck down Texas's sodomy laws and decriminalized same-sex acts nationwide.

State courts started to recognize more LGBT rights over the following years. Massachusetts's top court legalized same-sex unions in 2004, followed by courts in Connecticut in 2008 and Iowa in 2009. Same-sex marriage wasn't yet legal in Colorado in 2012, but Craig and Mullins planned to get married in Massachusetts and hold a reception in Colorado. Although almost unthinkable a decade earlier, gay rights activists were going to court and winning at a surprising speed.

Kennedy then wrote the majority opinion in *United States v. Windsor,* the 5–4 decision in 2013 that struck down the Defense of Marriage Act that defined marriage federally as between one man and one woman. And he joined the liberal wing again for a 5–4 decision in *Obergefell v. Hodges,* the 2015 case that legalized same-sex marriage nationwide.

But Kennedy also had expressed a need to tolerate religious beliefs, including in that majority opinion he authored in *Obergefell.* The Supreme Court ruled that it was demeaning to lock same-sex couples out of marriage, a central institution of society, especially when viewed against the long backdrop of disapproval of their relationships. Yet Kennedy's majority opinion acknowledged the other side, stating that the view that marriage is between one man and one woman "long has been held—and continues to be held—in good faith by reasonable and sincere people here and throughout the world."

When it came to considering the issue in the *Masterpiece Cakeshop* case, the Supreme Court had turned aside similar cases in the past, including a 2014 case concerning whether New Mexico's courts were correct to rule against a photographer who refused to work a same-sex commitment ceremony.

Masterpiece Cakeshop would press Kennedy to decide whether gay rights would have to give way in the face of sincere religious beliefs, or vice versa.

Kennedy's pivotal role was not lost on the social and legal groups who had elevated this case, shaped it, and brought it to the Supreme Court. A heavyweight battle like this can be costly, take years, and depend on experienced lawyering.

It all started when Craig and Mullins posted on Facebook about their experience and filed a complaint with the Colorado Civil Rights Commission in 2012. Phillips had declined to make a custom cake for the gay couple. The commission would rule that Phillips and his shop could not refuse to sell to same-sex couples any product that he would sell to heterosexual couples. For Phillips, this meant either losing roughly 40 percent of his income from selling custom wedding cakes or, in his view, being forced to participate in same-sex weddings against his beliefs. His case would later be taken up by Alliance Defending Freedom, a well-funded and politically connected conservative legal group that fought in other high-profile religious rights cases, including against same-sex marriage in *Obergefell*.

The commission's decision prompted heated pushback from religious individuals and groups. Phillips said he got death threats, but at the same time his business doubled with customers who supported his stance. Craig and Mullins said they received an outpouring of support. Activists who opposed same-sex marriage called gay-friendly bakeries and ordered cakes proclaiming their views, an effort to highlight their point that religious rights were at stake, not just LGBT rights.

One of those activists was William Jack, whose actions would become central in the case. Jack, a Colorado citizen and self-described Christian educator who teaches nationally, went into Le Bakery Sensual and two other Denver bakeries in 2014. He asked for two custom cakes in the shape of open Bibles, each with an image of two groomsmen, holding hands, with a red 'X' over the image, with the following messages: "God hates sin. Psalm 45:7" and "Homosexuality is a detestable sin. Leviticus 18:2." The bakeries refused, and Jack filed discrimination claims with the state commission. The commission ruled that those bakers didn't have to make the anti–same-sex marriage cakes Jack ordered. Jack called it a glaring inconsistency with the commission's decision about Masterpiece Cakeshop. Jack would later tell the Supreme Court in a brief that he was subject to unequal treatment from the state based on his affirmation of Christianity.

Chapter 2

Craig and Mullins, backed by the American Civil Liberties Union (ACLU), along with a host of civil rights groups, argued that businesses open to the general public must sell their products and services under the same terms and conditions to everyone, regardless of the owner's religion or the customer's sexual orientation. They relied on a principle that goes back to the Supreme Court's landmark 1968 decision about racial discrimination in businesses, *Newman v. Piggie Park*. In that case, three black customers went to the Piggie Park barbeque restaurant in South Carolina, but the owner refused to allow them to use a drive-in, as the NAACP Legal Defense and Educational Fund described it in a brief. The owner believed that serving black customers or contributing to racial intermixing in any way contravened "the will of God." The owner allowed black customers to purchase food only if they didn't eat at the restaurant. The Supreme Court unanimously ruled that businesses can't racially discriminate in that way, and the civil rights groups argued that should equally apply today to gay customers.

What made *Masterpiece Cakeshop* trickier, however, is that Phillips argued that he was not simply making a cake but that it was a custom cake that constituted artistic expression. "Much like an artist sketching on canvas or a sculptor using clay, Phillips meticulously crafts each wedding cake through hours of sketching, sculpting, and hand-painting," Phillips's attorneys said in the brief. "The cake, which serves as the iconic centerpiece of the marriage celebration, announces through Phillips's voice that a marriage has occurred and should be celebrated."

If the justices considered the cakes as art, it would trigger significant First Amendment concerns that he was being compelled to speak in a way that countered his religious beliefs. If Phillips's cakes were just cakes, however, it might not trigger the same constitutional concerns.

And that's why the Supreme Court got picture after picture of cakes in briefs filed in the case, trying to convince them that a custom cake is expressive. "Until now," a group of eleven cake makers said in a brief, "this Court has not had the opportunity to think that deeply about that kind of cake." Custom cakes, specially crafted with a particular client's needs in mind, are "utterly different" from cakes meant to be sold to any buyer, the cake makers told the court. And to prove it, they included images of custom cakes in the shapes of different scenes: a cowboy riding a pig, a lobster climbing from a steaming pot, a city bus—and, of course, wedding cakes.

A group of Republican lawmakers stressed to the justices that a custom wedding cake is protected speech under the First Amendment because the design and the cake itself say something and have meaning. "Cake carries within itself a message of bounty and plenty," the lawmaker brief stated. "The cake's message transcends food."

At the oral arguments, the court's liberals expressed concern about what other types of businesses could say they are artists and, therefore, claim they do not have to serve gay customers. If wedding-cake baking is an art form, what about a floral arrangement, Justice Ruth Bader Ginsburg asked? Or the design of wedding invitations, or the menu for the wedding dinner? The justices were searching for where to draw a line because if the court ruled that Phillips was an artist in baking his cakes, it would invite a series of lawsuits in which the court would have to decide which professions are artistic and, therefore, protected in their choice not to work a same-sex wedding.

Justice Elena Kagan pressed Phillips's lawyer, Kristen Waggoner, about a makeup artist, or a hairstylist. Why wouldn't they also count? "Because it's not speech," Waggoner replied. Kagan shot back: "Some people may say that about cakes, you know?" Justice Sonia Sotomayor was blunt about the idea of extending First Amendment protections to food. "In the end, its only purpose is to be eaten," Sotomayor said.

Noel Francisco, the solicitor general arguing on behalf of the Trump administration, took the side of the baker. He said that requiring Phillips to bake a cake was like compelling "an African American sculptor to sculpt a cross for the Klan service just because he'd do it for other religions." Or "a gay opera singer to perform at the Westboro Baptist Church just because that opera singer would be willing to perform at the National Cathedral."

But all eyes and ears were on Kennedy. He pressed lawyers on both sides in a way that showed how divided he was in his thinking on the case. First, he expressed some of the same reservations about how wide a swath the Supreme Court would cut into anti-discrimination laws if the justices determined a cake was a work art. He told Francisco that many of the examples of other professionals involved in ceremonies—such as a wedding photographer—do involve artistic speech. He worried that siding with Phillips would give companies the ability to boycott gay marriages.

"What would the government's position be if you prevail in this case, the baker prevails in this case, and then bakers all over the country received urgent requests: Please do not bake cakes for gay weddings," Kennedy said. "And more and more bakers began to comply. Would the government feel vindicated in its position that it now submits to us?" He then asked Francisco, if the government prevailed, "could the baker put a sign in his window, we do not bake cakes for gay weddings? And you would not think that an affront to the gay community?"

But Kennedy's remarks later in the argument suggested he was also concerned by the actions of the state commission. Kennedy referred to a comment from one of the commissioners who decided the Phillips case, who said that freedom of religion, when it is used to justify discrimination, is a "despicable" piece of rhetoric.

Kennedy asked the attorney defending Colorado's decision against Phillips, Frederick Yarger, to disavow the statement. "Suppose we thought that in significant part at least one member of the Commission based the commissioner's decision on the grounds of hostility to religion. Could your judgment then stand?" Kennedy asked. And later, Kennedy interjected with a statement on tolerance of religion. "Counselor, tolerance is essential in a free society. And tolerance is most meaningful when it's mutual. It seems to me that the state in its position here has been neither tolerant nor respectful of Mr. Phillips' religious beliefs."

To no one's surprise, Kennedy wrote the court's opinion. But the decision stopped frustratingly short of resolving the main questions in the case. Instead, Kennedy and the court focused on the "hostility" of the state when ruling against Phillips. Kennedy wrote that the commissioner had disparaged Phillips's religion by calling it "despicable" and using the word "rhetoric," which characterizes it as something "insubstantial and even insincere." The sentiment "is inappropriate for a Commission charged with the solemn responsibility of fair and neutral enforcement of Colorado's anti-discrimination law—a law that protects against discrimination on the basis of religion as well as sexual orientation."

To that point, Kennedy also highlighted the difference in how the commission ruled against Phillips in his refusal to make a same-sex wedding cake, while ruling in favor of the three bakeries that refused to make cakes sought by Jack that conveyed disapproval of same-sex marriage.

So the court, in a 7–2 opinion that threw out the Colorado commission's decision, opted to send a strong message that states can't show any sign of hostility to religion when deciding whether a business owner violates anti-discrimination laws. Otherwise, the court left the underlying issue up to the states for now.

"The outcome of cases like this in other circumstances must await further elaboration in the courts, all in the context of recognizing that these disputes must be resolved with tolerance, without undue disrespect to sincere religious beliefs, and without subjecting gay persons to indignities when they seek goods and services in an open market," Kennedy wrote.

The Supreme Court did little to shape how those lower courts should draw a line about when a cake becomes a work of art that deserves First Amendment protections. The opinion essentially stuck to the facts of how the commission treated Phillips's case. There was some limited guidance from the court. Kennedy wrote that states can pass laws to protect gay people from discrimination. And he said clergy who object to gay marriage on religious grounds could not be compelled to perform a ceremony under those laws. But all the other businesses fall somewhere in between, and the court declined to say where.

Kennedy basically described the difficult decision facing the court in the future. "Any decision in favor of the baker would have to be sufficiently constrained, lest all purveyors of goods and services who object to gay marriages for moral and religious reasons in effect be allowed to put up signs saying 'no goods or services will be sold if they will be used for gay marriages,' something that would impose a serious stigma on gay persons," Kennedy wrote.

Sotomayor and Ginsburg authored a dissent that pointed out that the commission was not the only one to review Phillips's case, so the comments of one commissioner should not negate the entire outcome of the case. While the deliberations between the justices took place behind closed doors, the decision appeared to be Kennedy's, with the rest of the justices following along. Kagan and Justice Neil Gorsuch wrote their own concurring opinions to battle over how the state commission could have justified treating Phillips differently from the bakers who turned down Jack, foreshadowing some of the arguments that could be made when a similar case comes to the Supreme Court in the future.

The Supreme Court had another case teed up on this issue that it could have chosen to hear next term. A florist in Washington state argued that she could refuse to provide floral arrangements for a same-sex wedding. The justices sent that case back to the lower courts to review whether there was religious hostility in that ruling as well. The ACLU says there is none to be found.

With the major questions left unsettled, both sides of the debate found reasons to declare victory.

Waggoner, Phillips's attorney, said the decision "makes clear that the government must respect [Phillips's] beliefs about marriage." Kim Colby of the Christian Legal Society's Center for Law and Religious Freedom called the ruling in favor of Phillips "an essential win for religious freedom" because the court didn't shut the door on such claims. The next business owner who brings a similar claim would have a viable argument, Colby indicated: "The court basically hit a reset button on sort of the disrespect for religious freedom that we've been seeing in the last five years. . . . And I think today's decision is a call for a pluralistic society in which all Americans have the right to live according to their deepest beliefs, values, and convictions."

James Esseks of the ACLU, which represented Craig and Mullins, said that although the court sided with the baker, it did so in a way that was so narrow it would not apply to future cases. "But the court has clearly signaled that the broader rule the bakery was seeking here—a constitutional right to discriminate and turn customers away because of who they are—is not in keeping with American constitutional tradition," Esseks wrote.

Within weeks, state courts in Arizona, Oregon, and Hawaii had ruled against businesses that declined to serve gay customers. The Oregon case was about a bakery that refused to make a wedding cake for a lesbian couple in 2013. The lawyers for the bakers in that case told *The*

Oregonian that they would be asking the U.S. Supreme Court to step in and bring clarity to the issue.

In the *Masterpiece Cakeshop* case, Kennedy and the other justices passed on an opportunity to settle a major social issue, and now the justices will have to decide whether to wade into the issue again—without Kennedy as the center of the court.

Chapter 3

How to Knock Down a Precedent

South Dakota's lawmakers spent the first few months of 2016 passing a measure that they knew would be struck down as unconstitutional. They designed it so that the law would end up in a legal fight quickly. Then, once in court, the state's lawyers conceded that previous U.S. Supreme Court rulings meant the law should not stand.

Why would South Dakota's legislature and governor bother to pass a law just to ensure its death by courts? Because a Supreme Court justice had invited them to do so months earlier.

Justice Anthony M. Kennedy went out of his way to call for a case that would allow the justices to reconsider two old Supreme Court decisions about states collecting taxes from online sales. Kennedy, in a 2015 case, on a different but related issue, wrote that those decisions from decades ago were "inflicting extreme harm and unfairness" on South Dakota and other states that are unable to collect billions of dollars in tax revenue annually needed for schools, health care, and roads.

"The legal system should find an appropriate case for this Court to reexamine" the two cases from 1967 and 1992, Kennedy wrote. Within days, a lawyer from a law firm in Washington, D.C. that specializes in Supreme Court cases helped South Dakota draft a bill that would be as appetizing as possible to the justices. Within months, state officials did their work and sent the case into the court system.

Three years after Kennedy's call, the Supreme Court sided with the state in *South Dakota v. Wayfair Inc.* during the 2017 October Term, reversing the court's precedents in a decision expected to create significant changes in online retail businesses, which have become a large sector of the nation's economy.

The *Wayfair* case highlights a way that Supreme Court justices can proactively call for cases that allow them to eliminate longstanding prior decisions with which they disagree, allowing the court to use its power to reshape the nation's business landscape even if other justices say such complex economic issues are best left to Congress.

The 5–4 vote also provides a clear illustration of how and when Chief Justice John G. Roberts Jr. will depart from the views of the other conservative justices on respecting the court's prior rulings and defer to Congress—even when he agrees that the previous ruling was wrong.

Advocacy groups already have pointed to the case as a path to attack precedents that they want to see reversed, including The Family Foundation and others that want to undo the landmark 1973 ruling in *Roe v. Wade* that established a constitutional right to an abortion.

"The Wayfair case today has demonstrated that precedent can be overturned," Sean Maguire, grassroots coordinator for the Virginia anti-abortion group, wrote. "The word from the Supreme Court is not final. *Roe v. Wade* will not stand forever."

The central issue in the *Wayfair* case might not come close to evoking the same passion as the abortion debate, but it is hugely important for the vast majority of states and for setting the terms of the business climate that has allowed Amazon, eBay, and other online retailers to flourish online.

It starts with poor South Dakota—literally. Along with forty-four other states and the District of Columbia, South Dakota relies on a "sales and use taxes" structure as an efficient way to collect money for road construction, health care, and other essential government functions. This works well when someone in South Dakota buys, say, a bicycle at a brick-and-mortar store on Main Street, because stores with a "physical presence" in the state are required to collect the sales tax owed at the time of the purchase. The customer rides out the door without having to write down or remember to pay the taxes, and then the stores send the tax to the state. Easy and effective.

But this doesn't work when someone in South Dakota buys that bicycle from an online retailer in another state that doesn't have a physical presence in the state. South Dakota and other states stood powerless to force those out-of-state retailers to collect taxes for online sales because of *Quill Corp. v. North Dakota,* a Supreme Court decision from 1992, about two years before the first online purchase was ever made. This was no small problem for governments and mom-and-pop shops alike. South Dakota has no income tax, so the state raises around 60 percent of its revenue from sales taxes. Stores operating in South

Dakota have, therefore, been at a competitive disadvantage to out-of-state retailers who do not have to add the state's 4.5 percent sales tax to the price of products.

The pain inflicted has become more severe over time, as more customers have turned to the Internet to shop from the comfort of their own homes and have found better prices and wider selection than they do at the store down the street. State losses from e-commerce were $7 billion in 2009 and $23 billion in 2012, according to two studies cited in a brief by states that had the same problems as South Dakota. Their brief in the case gave a few examples: Alabama cut $17 million from its state court budget in 2012, when $170 million in sales tax from e-commerce purchases went uncollected, while New York eliminated $337 million from Medicaid spending that same year when its uncollected taxes from online sales amounted to $865 million. Adding to the squeeze: if states raised sales taxes to raise more funds, they'd risk driving even more customers online to avoid paying them. Despite this concern, South Dakota lawmakers felt compelled to raise the state sales tax by half of a percent in 2016 to help pay to increase teacher salaries.

One potential but unlikely solution was Congress. The Supreme Court in the *Quill* case had invited lawmakers to step in and address interstate sales and use taxes. But Congress, which was well aware of the fate of South Dakota and other states, had accomplished nothing to resolve the issue for twenty-five years. That left South Dakota to look to the Supreme Court. The state would have to convince the justices to abandon *stare decisis*—the tradition of leaving in place a prior ruling unless there is a good reason to overturn it—and get rid of their own ruling in *Quill*. One of the hurdles was that the court in *Quill* had heavily relied on *stare decisis* to uphold a 1967 decision that first established the physical presence requirement, *National Bellas Hess, Inc. v. Department of Revenue of Illinois*.

The weight of fifty years of established Supreme Court precedent would have to be lifted. And to do that, Kennedy would need to change his mind.

Kennedy, back in 1992, voted with the majority in *Quill* to uphold the physical presence requirement established in *Bellas Hess*. He did this based on *stare decisis* alone, joining part of the opinion that put a special emphasis on why it is important to uphold the court's prior decisions.

The issues then were almost parallel to those in the South Dakota case of this term, if you were to rewind technology by twenty-five years. At the time, North Dakota sought to get rid of the "physical presence" standard to force out-of-state mail-order businesses who were selling to residents to collect taxes on sales. The mail-order business had turned "from a relatively inconsequential market niche" in 1967 to a "goliath" in 1982, and advances in computer technology made it easier for businesses in other parts of the country to comply with the state's taxing scheme. North Dakota wanted the court to overturn its own ruling in *Bellas Hess*.

The Supreme Court declined to do so in *Quill*. A quick detour into a strange part of the Supreme Court's relationship with the Constitution's Commerce Clause is necessary to explain why. That clause authorizes Congress to "regulate Commerce with foreign Nations, and among the several States," but is silent about the regulation of interstate commerce in the absence of any action by Congress. The court over the years has stepped into that role in various ways when Congress hasn't seized that power, particularly when it comes to state laws that the court decides unduly interfere with interstate commerce.

In *Quill,* the court ruled that the physical presence rule was necessary under the Commerce Clause to prevent such undue burdens. Justice John Paul Stevens, writing for the majority, said there was value of "a bright line rule in this area and the doctrine and principles of stare decisis indicate that the *Bellas Hess* rule remains good law." The court then invited Congress to act, since lawmakers "may be better qualified to resolve" the issue. "Congress is now free to decide whether, when, and to what extent the States may burden interstate mail order concerns with a duty to collect use taxes," Stevens wrote.

Kennedy, along with Justice Clarence Thomas, joined a concurrence written by Justice Antonin Scalia that underscored the importance of *stare decisis*—in fact, that was the only reason they voted with the majority to keep the physical presence requirement. Kennedy had been on the court for four years at that point, and Thomas for just one year.

Scalia's concurrence covered the areas that were important to *stare decisis.* First, Congress has the final say over the regulation of interstate commerce and can change the rule of *Bellas Hess* simply by saying so, a situation that means the doctrine of *stare decisis* has a "special force." Second, businesses have relied on the *Bellas Hess* decision as part of the basic framework of a sizeable industry, and the *stare decisis* doctrine is at its peak when a decision is relied on in such a way. Scalia also underscored how the court's reputation was at stake.

"It seems to me important that we retain our ability—and, what comes to the same thing, that we maintain public confidence in our ability—sometimes to adopt new principles for the resolution of new issues without abandoning clear holdings of the past that those principles contradict," Scalia wrote. The court in other cases had suggested that the physical presence rule from *Bellas Hess* would stick around, Scalia wrote, and "we ought not visit economic hardship upon those who took us at our word."

Congress failed to act over the next two decades, although it had tried almost continuously.

Kennedy apparently changed his mind on *Quill* in the meantime, and expressed as much in a 2015 case. The court decided to uphold a Colorado law that sought to get around the *Quill* and *Bellas Hess* decisions by forcing online retailers to report sales to the state. Kennedy wrote separately in that case—calling it appropriate and necessary to do so— that "there is a powerful case to be made" for getting rid of the physical presence rule in *Quill*. That the *Quill* decision kept that standard "on stare decisis alone" underscored "the tenuous nature of that holding," Kennedy wrote. Unlike the situation in 1992, current-day shoppers have almost instant access to most retailers via cell phones and laptops, so a business can be present in a state "without presence being physical in the traditional sense of the term."

"Given these changes in technology and consumer sophistication, it is unwise to delay any longer a reconsideration of the Court's holding in *Quill*," Kennedy wrote. "A case questionable even when decided, *Quill* now harms States to a degree far greater than could have been anticipated earlier."

South Dakota answered that call.

The Supreme Court's oral arguments in April 2018 highlighted the deep divide on the bench over *stare decisis,* particularly the principles highlighted in the *Quill* decision. The discussion centered not on whether the previous ruling was a mistake but on whether Congress or the Supreme Court should fix it.

Kennedy, in the 2015 case, clearly had signaled his intent to get rid of *Quill*. Thomas, who was critical of the court's approach to the Commerce Clause in a 2003 opinion, likely would be on that side as well. And Neil Gorsuch, now a justice, had written critically of the court's Commerce Clause decisions in that same Colorado case from 2015 when he was a judge on the U.S. Court of Appeals for the Tenth Circuit.

The chances that Congress would act certainly were unclear. Some lawmakers who had worked on the issue for more than two decades had filed a brief urging the court to overturn *Quill* because that would prompt Congress to act. Other lawmakers asked the court to stay out of it because negotiations were ongoing on several current bills.

House Judiciary Committee Chairman Robert W. Goodlatte, R-Va., attended the arguments and filed a brief arguing that states failed to get their way in Congress and were now trying to use the court to bypass the legislative process. Goodlatte was right in the thick of the discussions in 2014 on a legislative push to overturn *Quill* that fell short.

"This tests the court's commitment to the rule of law—not just the particular rule of law announced but to *stare decisis*," Goodlatte and other lawmakers said in their brief. "South Dakota and its amici—including the Solicitor General—all approach this case as if this Court truly was their last resort. It isn't. Congress is the branch of government constitutionally entrusted to decide whether the physical presence rule of *Bellas Hess* should stay or go."

Chapter 3

With Goodlatte watching silently in the gallery, Marty Jackley, the attorney general for South Dakota, countered that view during arguments. Jackley said the justices should act because it was not Congress but the *Quill* decision that was preventing the collection of taxes.

Justice Elena Kagan pushed back on that idea several times, pointing out that the choice for the court was to either keep or ditch the rule, while Congress can craft compromises and balance the wide range of interests involved in the case.

"This is not the kind of issue where you say: Well, probably didn't get on Congress's radar screen or maybe Congress was too busy doing other things," Kagan said at one point. "This is a very prominent issue which Congress has been aware of for a very long time and has chosen not to do something about that. And that seems to make your bar higher to surmount, isn't it?"

Other justices raised more practical issues about the problems of the court's acting before Congress on the *Quill* decision. Roberts at one point highlighted how the problem appeared to have peaked because, among other reasons, bigger e-commerce companies have a physical presence in all fifty states and so are covered and already paying taxes. "And, if it is, in fact, a problem that is diminishing rather than expanding, why doesn't that suggest that there are greater significance to the arguments that we should leave *Quill* in place?" Roberts asked.

Justice Sonia Sotomayor, meanwhile, asserted that overturning *Quill* would bring up a whole host of questions and uncertainty. "What happens when the tax program breaks down, as it already has for the states who are using it, and merchants can't keep track of who they've sold to?" Sotomayor asked. "All of these are questions that are fraught with difficulties. So you're introducing now a whole new set of difficulties to put behind something that's been in place for 30 years now?"

The court appeared deeply split: Should it keep a more reserved role when it comes to a big economic policy question, since Congress is free to act and better suited to come up with a nuanced policy?

Kennedy seemed to have made up his mind years ago, and the court went his way. Four justices joined him for a 5–4 decision that focused on the court's role in the government. Conservative justices Thomas, Gorsuch, and Samuel A. Alito Jr. took his side, along with the liberal Ruth Bader Ginsburg, and they brushed aside the concerns about *stare decisis* in this case.

Kennedy, writing the majority, said the Supreme Court made the mess, so it should clean it up. He said the *Quill* and *Bellas Hess* decisions created a physical presence rule that is harming the states and causing major market distortions, so the court's "proper role" isn't to ask Congress to fix those precedents, particularly now that they are further removed from the economic realities of the Internet age. Also, the purpose of the Commerce Clause is not to allow the judiciary to create "artificial" distortions in the business environment, he wrote.

"*Quill* has come to serve as a judicially created tax shelter for businesses that limit their physical presence and still sell their goods to a state's consumers, and that has become easier and more prevalent as technology has advanced," Kennedy wrote. "Rejecting the physical presence rule is necessary to ensure that artificial competitive advantages are not created by this court's precedents."

Kennedy further attacked the pillars of *stare decisis* in the case, quoting a 2009 opinion that "stare decisis is not an inexorable command." Courts have acted as the front line of review in this limited sphere of interstate commerce, Kennedy wrote, and it is important that their principles be accurate and logical "whether or not Congress can or will act in response."

The justices that decided *Quill* in 1992 did not know and couldn't have envisioned the present realities of the interstate marketplace in which the world's largest retailer is a remote seller, Kennedy wrote. At the time fewer than 2 percent of Americans had Internet access, and mail-order sales in the United States totaled $180 billion. By 2018 those numbers were about 89 percent and $454 billion, respectively.

And state statutes that try to fix this issue "are likely to embroil courts in technical and arbitrary disputes about what counts as physical presence," Kennedy wrote. When it comes to businesses that rely on the *Quill* decision, the physical presence rule "is no longer a clear or easily applicable standard, so arguments for reliance based on its clarity are misplaced."

The *Quill* court was wrong to uphold the 1967 physical presence standard from *Bellas Hess*, Kennedy wrote, and courts "should be vigilant in correcting the error."

Roberts, writing for the dissenters, said that a past mistake from 1967—and it was a mistake—doesn't mean the court should act on an important question of current economic policy just to correct it. He wrote that the majority opinion disregards the costs that its decision will impose on retailers, particularly on small businesses, and how this could dampen opportunities for commerce in a broad range of new markets.

"E-commerce has grown into a significant and vibrant part of our national economy against the backdrop of established rules, including the physical-presence rule," Roberts wrote. "Any alteration to those rules with the potential to disrupt the development of such a critical segment of the economy should be undertaken by Congress."

Lawmakers have been free to replace those rules at any time with legislation of their own, he added. "A good reason to leave these matters to Congress is that legislators may more directly consider the competing interests at stake," Roberts wrote. "Unlike this Court, Congress has the flexibility to address these questions in a wide variety of ways."

Roberts underscored that the court shouldn't overturn its precedents lightly and that the bar is even higher when Congress can act in that area. Suddenly changing the ground rules may waylay Congress's consideration of the issue because state officials will redirect their attention from working with Congress on a national solution to securing new tax revenue from remote retailers.

"This is neither the first, nor the second, but the third time this Court has been asked whether a State may obligate sellers with no physical presence within its borders to collect tax on sales to residents," Roberts wrote. "Whatever salience the adage 'third time's a charm' has in daily life, it is a poor guide to Supreme Court decisionmaking."

It was only the second dissent Roberts wrote all term.

Court watchers say the *Wayfair* reasoning weakened the principle of *stare decisis* for future rulings and invited similar challenges—as well as established a blueprint for reversing a Supreme Court ruling with a plainly unconstitutional law and fast-track appeal.

"South Dakota's success would surely embolden numerous other actors to try the same stunt," a brief from the Americans for Tax Reform warned the justices in the *Wayfair* case. "Unfortunately, it takes little imagination to think of efforts in other arenas that could quickly yield dangerous stand-offs in state capitals and state courts across the country."

Some examples the group gave: aggressive libel laws allowing prosecutors to bring charges against journalists for publishing inaccurate reports to challenge existing First Amendment rulings, or aggressive gun-restriction laws that try to force a new review of the scope of the Second Amendment.

Kennedy, for someone whose legacy on the court rests on 5–4 decisions, might have reinforced the very arguments that a new conservative majority could use to strip away his most noted decisions, George Washington University law professor Jonathan Turley wrote in the *Washington Post*.

"Kennedy once said, 'Sometimes you don't know if you're Caesar about to cross the Rubicon or Captain Queeg cutting your own tow line,'" Turley said. "This is certainly one of those moments."

Chapter 4

Privacy in the Digital Age

Americans don't really have a choice these days but to carry a cell phone—or two. The Supreme Court first recognized this in a 2014 decision, in which the justices concluded that more than 90 percent of the country's adults carried a cell phone containing photos, e-mails, and a digital record of nearly every aspect of their lives. The court back then required police to get a warrant to search a cell phone seized during an arrest—a major step to protect the privacy rights of Americans amid the ongoing march into the digital age.

But information stored on a cell phone is only part of the story when it comes to what the data can tell about its user. There's also the information a phone sends to the cell phone companies—a regular ping to radio towers to make sure a call or text can get through. The cell phone companies collect those pings for various reasons. Those pings record someone's movements through the world. And federal investigators have turned to those cell phone company records to reveal where criminal suspects have been, sometimes for months at a time.

At the start of the 2017 October Term, the Supreme Court had not yet confronted whether police need to get a warrant before requesting that location data. A convicted bank robber, through the American Civil Liberties Union, was asking the justices to upend the court's decades-old precedents on the privacy of business records and reshape Americans' rights against increasing threats to privacy.

The Supreme Court's decision in *Carpenter v. United States* would divide the court but ultimately demonstrate that Chief Justice John G. Roberts Jr. wants the court to be a forward-looking defender of Fourth Amendment protections against government searches and seizures. To do so, he even needed to take the rare step of going against both the court's previous rulings and a reluctant conservative wing of the court.

The decision also shows how one justice, this time Sonia Sotomayor, can suggest that the Supreme Court as an institution change its direction in one area of the law and ultimately influence the court's view about how technology affects the daily lives of Americans.

"I don't think it's an exaggeration to say this is the most important Fourth Amendment case we've seen in a generation," Nathan Wessler, an ACLU staff lawyer, said ahead of the case. "It really promises to decide whether the mere use of modern technologies is going to make our lives into an open book for the government without the protections of a warrant."

Timothy Carpenter, the criminal defendant at the center of the case, is not the most compelling hero in the fight over privacy in the digital age. FBI agents in Detroit went to cell phone companies to obtain several months of records about Carpenter and other suspected armed robbers. The investigators wanted that data to determine whether the suspects had been in an area where crimes had been committed at the time they were committed. The 12,898 data points investigators got showed Carpenter's location at an average of 101 times a day for 127 days. It showed him near four robbery locations. A jury convicted him, and he was sentenced to 116 years in prison.

But this case was not really about the fate of Timothy Carpenter at all. The ACLU had seized on the case as a way to challenge the ease with which investigators got those records. Justice Samuel A. Alito Jr. highlighted this during an exchange with Wessler during oral argument: "Could I just ask you this question: Is any of this going to do any good for Mr. Carpenter?" The courtroom filled with knowing laughter because, well, it really wouldn't. Regardless of how the justices decided this issue, Carpenter's chances of having his conviction overturned were slim.

Instead, the ACLU's appeal focused on two different ways the Supreme Court viewed the growing amount of personal data in technology when it comes to the Fourth Amendment. On the one hand were court rulings from the 1970s that treated that information like typical business records. And on the other were more recent rulings that noted distinct privacy concerns about the police's collection of vast amounts of data about people via new technology such as the Global Positioning System, or GPS.

The U.S. Court of Appeals for the Sixth Circuit upheld Carpenter's conviction but noted concerns when it came to applying the two standards. FBI agents investigating Carpenter had used a federal law that governs business records to obtain the data about his whereabouts. They were allowed to do so because of 1970s rulings that established something called the "third-party" doctrine. That doctrine holds that a suspect (the first party) has no privacy rights to stop investigators (the second party) from searching and seizing records the suspect voluntarily gave to a business (a third party). That remains true even if the business records contain sensitive and revealing information, such as a history of credit card purchases held by a bank, as the Supreme Court ruled in 1976 in *United States v. Miller,* or a history of dialed telephone numbers held by a telephone company, as the Supreme Court ruled in 1979 in *Smith v. Maryland.*

Under those cases, investigators would need a warrant to search a cell phone, but they wouldn't need a warrant to get records from a third party. That meant they didn't need to convince a judge that there was probable cause to get the business records, which is a more difficult legal standard to meet. Two of the appeals court judges said that this standard still applied to records for cell phone location data.

But those judges also noted that the Supreme Court, in a 2012 case that divided the justices 5–4, found that people have a reasonable expectation of privacy with regard to longer-term monitoring of their movements in government investigations. In that decision, *United States v. Jones,* the Supreme Court ruled it was a search under the Fourth Amendment when investigators attached a GPS unit to a suspect's car to track its movements for almost a month.

One member of the appeals court panel that heard Carpenter's case, Judge Jane Stranch, wrote separately to point out that the cell phone location data the investigators got on Carpenter was as precise as GPS. She wrote in the case that the quantity of sensitive information the FBI received without a warrant in Carpenter's case raised the same type of privacy concerns that the Supreme Court raised in the *Jones* case. Treating the cell tower data simply as a "business record," she wrote, does not address concerns "regarding long-term, comprehensive tracking of an individual's location without a warrant."

The ACLU took the case to the Supreme Court.

None of this was new to Sotomayor, who first laid out the stakes of digital surveillance in the *Jones* case in 2012. Back then, the Supreme Court was just starting to grapple with the police's use of new technology that could track individuals. The *Jones* decision in 2012 looms large because the justices expressed for the first time real concerns about how much the government could learn about Americans through technology. The court sided with a drug dealer whose Jeep had been tracked by investigators who planted a GPS device on his car. But Sotomayor went further in the case, penning a separate concurrence that took dead aim at the two rulings from the 1970s that form the heart of the third-party doctrine, even though they weren't at issue in the case.

Sotomayor focused on the presumed privacy of a person's movements when it comes to ever-present technology such as GPS, particularly when it involves the government's acquiring that information without any oversight from the judicial branch. Movements can reveal what church people go to, what meetings they attend, and where they spend their nights. "I would ask whether people reasonably expect that their movements will be recorded and aggregated in a manner that enables the Government to ascertain, more or less at will, their political and religious beliefs, sexual habits, and so on," Sotomayor wrote.

The court should reconsider the premise that an individual has no reasonable expectation of privacy in information voluntarily disclosed to third parties, Sotomayor wrote. "This approach is ill-suited to the digital age, in which people reveal a great deal of information about themselves to third parties in the course of carrying out mundane tasks," Sotomayor wrote. "People disclose phone numbers that they dial or text to their cellular providers; the URLs that they visit and the e-mail addresses with which they correspond to their internet service providers; and the books, groceries, and medications they purchase to online retailers."

Not all information voluntarily disclosed to some business for a limited purpose should lose Fourth Amendment protections, Sotomayor wrote.

The suggestion was strikingly forward-looking. No other justice joined it. But the chief justice soon would take notice.

The court has seemed a bit aloof when it comes to emerging technology, a sign of how cloistered the justices are in their marble building on Capitol Hill. Justice Elena Kagan, in a 2013 speech reported by the Associated Press, told an audience that technologies such as Facebook, Twitter, and e-mail are "a challenge for us." Roberts, during oral arguments, called an Internet search site a "search station," and Sotomayor asked how Dropbox is similar to "iDrop in the cloud," which is something that doesn't exist, according to an *Ars Technica* article that compiled a list of times at oral arguments that the justices revealed some lack of tech savvy.

In 2014, Roberts and Scalia drew howls from court observers for seeming like tech neophytes during the next big digital privacy case after *Jones, Riley v. California,* about whether police could search the cell phones of people they arrested without getting a warrant. Roberts questioned why anyone but drug dealers would have two cell phones. And when the lawyer said many people carry two cell phones, and that she knew that simply because of observation, Scalia replied: "You've observed different people from the people that I've observed." It was an exchange that Sotomayor would later use an example of the importance of personal experience in shaping legal opinions.

"In a room full of government lawyers, each one of them has two cell phones," NBC reported Sotomayor to have said to the crowd at a liberal American Constitution Society event. The crowd laughed.

"That's why it's important to have people with different life experiences," Sotomayor said. "Especially on a court like the Supreme Court, because we have to correct each other from misimpressions."

Tech questions had been sorted out by the time the justices issued the ruling in *Riley,* which required police to get a warrant to search the cell phone in the pocket of arrestees. The ruling nods to such terms as "there's an app for that," and notes the ubiquity of cell phones by saying "the proverbial visitor from Mars might conclude they were an important feature of human anatomy." The justices also did a thorough job in describing how a cell phone is a "minicomputer" that has photos, tape recorders, maps, rolodexes, diaries, and more that allow for a much larger invasion of privacy than a search of a physical item such as a cigarette box.

Roberts, writing for the majority, also concluded that the data on a cell phone is qualitatively different in part because it can reveal where a person has been. Historic location data is a standard feature on many smart phones, he noted, that can reconstruct someone's specific movements down to the minute, not only around town but in a particular building.

To make the point about why it is so important to acknowledge that such data can reveal details about familial, political, professional, religious, and sexual associations, Roberts cited Sotomayor's concurrence from the *Jones* case.

In the *Carpenter* case, the justices were clearly divided along ideological lines at oral arguments. Justices Anthony M. Kennedy and Samuel A. Alito Jr. made clear in several statements that they did not seem interested in throwing out the third-party doctrine that was such a settled part of Supreme Court precedent. Alito asked why cell location records would be considered more sensitive than bank records that list all of someone's purchases, even if the cell phone recorded data on a minute-to-minute basis.

At one point, Kennedy nodded with self-effacing humor about the court's relative ignorance about expectations for privacy in the digital era, saying that "there's a much more normal expectation that businesses have your cell phone data. I think everybody, almost everybody, knows that. If I know it, everybody does."

Sotomayor clearly had her eyes fixed on the future. Right now we're only talking about the records the companies keep about location data, Sotomayor said. "But as I understand it, a cell phone can be pinged in your bedroom. It can be pinged at your doctor's office. It can ping you in the most intimate details of your life. Presumably at some point even in a dressing room as you're undressing. So I am not beyond the belief that someday a provider could turn on my cell phone and listen to my conversations."

Kagan said the line of cases from the 1970s was developed when third parties didn't receive the kind of detailed information that cell phone companies get today. Michael Dreeben, the deputy solicitor general arguing for the government, insisted that these were the same types of business records considered in the 1970s cases. He told Kagan that Americans voluntarily decide to contract with a cell company.

Roberts interjected: "That sounds inconsistent with our decision in *Riley,* though, which emphasized that you really don't have a choice these days if you want to have a cell phone."

The exchange teased that Roberts appeared to be open to Sotomayor's suggestion from six years earlier that the third-party doctrine might not be a good fit for the digital age.

Before the 2017 October Term, there were only two times the chief justice had broken from his fellow conservatives and sided with the court's liberals to deliver a 5–4 majority, according to Adam Feldman, a postdoctoral fellow at Columbia Law School and creator of a high court statistics blog, *Empirical SCOTUS.*

One of them was among the most important cases in recent memory. Roberts in 2012 infuriated Republicans and the conservative wing when he voted with the liberal justices to uphold the 2010 health care law called the Affordable Care Act, or Obamacare.

After initially siding with the conservatives, Roberts had switched sides, and the reasons why had to do with his view of the role of the chief justice, according to Jeffrey Rosen, president and chief executive officer of the National Constitution Center. Rosen wrote in *The New Republic* in 2012 that he had interviewed Roberts years earlier about his philosophy about being chief justice. Roberts had expressed a desire to return the bipartisan legitimacy of the court, saying it had issued too many 5–4 decisions, and a test for the chief justice was promoting consensus for the court's long-term institutional interest.

In the Obamacare decision, Rosen saw Roberts as emphasizing Congress's broad powers to solve national problems, and the importance of the Supreme Court's deferring to Congress's policy choices. "All of these instincts converged in the health care case, in which Roberts set aside his ideological preference to protect the Court from a decision along party lines that would have imperiled its legitimacy," Rosen wrote.

In *Carpenter*, Roberts might have done something similar. He joined the liberal wing of the court for a 5–4 decision that punched a serious hole in the third-party doctrine and upset his fellow conservative justices. The majority ruled that customers have a Fourth Amendment right to protect cell phone location records held by a phone company, and so investigators need to have a warrant to search them.

In lengthy dissents, Alito and Kennedy hinted that they thought Roberts cut against the third-party doctrine out of a concern about the court's legacy when dealing with technology.

"The desire to make a statement about privacy in the digital age does not justify the consequences that today's decision is likely to produce," Alito wrote in a dissent. He predicted a "blizzard of litigation," a threat to valuable investigative techniques, and possibly the end of the third-party doctrine across the board. Giving individuals a privacy interest in any sensitive information collected about them by a third-party would count as a "revolutionary development," according to Alito. And it could prevent Congress from acting, even though legislation could provide broader privacy protections than the Fourth Amendment.

"If today's decision encourages the public to think that this Court can protect them from this looming threat to their privacy, the decision will mislead as well as disrupt," Alito wrote.

Kennedy hammered home the point that getting phone records from a company couldn't be considered a search of the person who owned the cell phone under the text of the Fourth Amendment—the records weren't in Carpenter's house, or in his phone, or in his possession in any way. Kennedy did not mince words: the majority is a "departure" from precedents. It draws "an unprincipled and unworkable line" between cell-site records on the one hand and financial and telephonic records on the other.

But Roberts, in the majority, kept his eye on the future instead of on those past precedents. "After all, when Smith was decided in 1979, few could have imagined a society in which a phone goes wherever its owner goes, conveying to the wireless carrier not just dialed digits, but a detailed and comprehensive record of the person's movements," Roberts wrote.

And Roberts called the cell site location information, or CSLI, "an entirely different species" of business record. "While the records in this case reflect the state of technology at the start of the decade, the accuracy of CSLI is rapidly approaching GPS-level precision," Roberts wrote.

Roberts ended with a nod to history and the role of the court. As Justice Louis Brandeis explained in a famous dissent, Roberts wrote, the court is obligated to ensure that the "progress of science" does not erode Fourth Amendment protections.

The majority's approach appears safe for the future, as well, particularly because Gorsuch wrote a dissent that essentially agreed with the majority's decision that 1970s cases should not apply to cell location information. Gorsuch went well beyond that to say the third-party doctrine in those cases is wrong—but then spent twenty pages searching for an answer he didn't quite come up with for how the court should treat this information.

"I do not begin to claim all the answers today," Gorsuch wrote, "but . . . at least I have a pretty good idea what the questions are."

Empowering the Presidency

The first week of Donald Trump's presidency demonstrated the country's deep social and political divisions. The day after the inauguration in January 2017, nearly half a million demonstrators filled the National Mall for a "Women's March on Washington." They carried signs objecting to Trump's crude language about "grabbing" women, but also questioned the president's seemingly too friendly relationship with Russian President Vladimir Putin, decried Trump's plan to build a wall on the U.S.-Mexico border, and generally commiserated about having him in the White House.

Trump used a speech at the CIA's wall of fallen heroes on his second day in office to chastise reports that the women's protest was larger than his inauguration. He also called members of the media "among the most dishonest human beings on Earth." Trump later ordered the wall to be built along the southern border. He insisted on his widely debunked claim that Democratic candidate Hillary Clinton won the popular vote only because of widespread voter fraud.

And at the end of that first week, on a Friday afternoon, Trump signed an executive order that blocked travelers from seven Muslim-majority countries from entering the United States. "I'm establishing new vetting measures to keep radical Islamic terrorists out of the United States of America. We don't want them here," Trump told the press cameras before signing the orders at the White House. In an unscripted remark minutes later, the president described one of the documents: "And this is the protection of the nation from foreign terrorist entry into the United States—we all know what that means."

Civil rights groups and some Democratic officials in the states believed they knew all too well "what that means." They filed lawsuits to stop what they said was a discriminatory and unlawful order to fulfill Trump's campaign promise to ban Muslims from entering the country.

Trump's efforts would become known simply as the travel ban. And for many in the country, the lawsuits became a test of whether the Supreme Court would restrain a president who appeared to delight in enflaming racial tensions, as he had with equivocating comments about violent white nationalist protests and professional football players who kneeled during the national anthem to raise awareness of police brutality against minorities.

The Supreme Court had to decide whether it should second-guess a president who claimed to be using his broad national security powers in immigration matters. That would sharply divide the justices on the role of the court and drag them into the ideological fight that was polarizing the country.

The case also forced the Supreme Court to face its previous failures to stop discriminatory presidential actions, such as the Japanese internment camps set up during the Roosevelt administration in World War II. The decision not to intervene in presidential orders to create those camps remains among the most shameful moments in the institution's history. Three children of the men whose infamous cases challenged those camps urged the justices to reject the Trump administration's arguments in the current case.

"If it were to accept the government's invitation here to abdicate its judicial responsibility, the Court would repeat its failures in those widely condemned cases," those descendants wrote.

By the time the Supreme Court was ready to settle the travel ban issue in 2018, the Trump administration was on its third version of the policy. The government gave up on the original version of the travel ban from January 2017 after federal judges prevented it from going into effect. A second version of the ban from March 2017 was partially blocked as it moved through the courts. The third version was issued in September 2017. This one was fundamentally different in how it was crafted and how it justified the travel restrictions.

The original ban was born from politics. In December 2015, just months before voting in the 2016 presidential primaries began, a masked gunman and his wife entered a holiday party for county health workers in San Bernardino, California, and opened fire. The assailants killed fourteen and wounded twenty-two in one of the deadliest mass shootings in American history, and investigators concluded that they were inspired by Islamic terrorists. Days later, Trump responded with an infamous campaign pledge "calling for a total and complete shutdown of Muslims entering the United States until our country's representatives can figure out what is going on."

In January, the immediate implementation of the first travel ban created chaos at airports, where authorities detained travelers amid mass confusion about who could enter the United States. Protesters went to airports, followed by volunteer immigration lawyers. They filed lawsuits to help people such as Haider Sameer Abdukhaleq Alshawi of Iraq, arriving on a visa to rejoin his wife and son, who were in Houston as refugees because their family's association with the U.S. military had made them targets for insurgents. The government detained Alshawi at John F. Kennedy airport in New York, and he faced the possibility of being shut out of the country and prevented from being reunited with his family. Federal judges in Alshawi's case and others blocked the policy nationwide.

In the months that followed, one federal appeals court looked at Trump's campaign statement and posts on Twitter and concluded that the versions of the travel ban were unconstitutional in how they targeted Muslims. Another federal court ruled that the executive orders exceeded Trump's authority under federal immigration laws.

But the Trump administration said a third version of the travel ban, a presidential proclamation, was different. The Justice Department argued the latest version was based on a multi-agency government review of how well countries complied with U.S. standards for vetting immigrants and refugees seeking to come to America. The review involved not just Trump's actions but those of a number of government officials—the acting secretary of Homeland Security, the secretaries of State and Defense, and the attorney general. Trump then indefinitely restricted U.S.

entry by citizens of eight countries whose governments did not provide enough information to assess travelers.

The government argued that the proclamation didn't mention religion. It was neutral on its face. And the restrictions on Muslim-majority nations were limited to countries that were previously designated by Congress or prior administrations as posing national security risks. On top of that, the vast majority of Muslims in the world lived in countries that were not banned.

"These differences confirm that the Proclamation is based on national-security and foreign-affairs objectives, not religious animus," the government told the Supreme Court. The government also argued that the lower courts that blocked this third version "would constrain the ability of this and all future Presidents to take measures to protect the Nation and achieve critical foreign-relations objectives."

Critics of the policy didn't buy the latest version as anything but a continuation of the original travel ban. They suggested that the government's review of vetting standards had come up with a virtually identical ban and that the process just tried to launder an unconstitutional and unlawful policy that still fell almost exclusively on Muslims. David Cole, the national legal director of the ACLU, which challenged all three versions of the ban, wrote in *The New York Review of Books* that the case also tested the Supreme Court's ability to check a president's power.

"The case most directly implicates the rights of Muslims, here and abroad, singled out for disfavored treatment by a president who promised to do just that as a candidate," Cole wrote. "But because the administration has argued that the court must blindly defer to the president, the dispute equally concerns the very role of the court in the separation of powers."

The Supreme Court could hardly avoid deciding such a high-profile case, and it was clear the justices would be seen as partisan by one side or the other. The divide was stark in the month after Trump created the original ban, with 89 percent of Democrats opposing it and 81 percent of Republicans supporting it, according to a Pew Research Center poll. Trump continued to drive a wedge between the two sides throughout the court battle over the case, in television interviews and on his Twitter account. He called the second and third versions of the ban "watered down" and "politically correct" versions. He alluded on Twitter to a fake story about Gen. John J. Pershing's killing Muslim insurgents with bullets dipped in pig's blood. He retweeted anti-Muslim videos.

Dozens of lawmakers, religious organizations, and civil rights groups urged the court to strike down the ban. The U.S. Conference of Catholic Bishops and other Catholic groups told the justices in a brief that such blatant religious discrimination is repugnant to the Catholic faith, core American values, and the Constitution, and "poses a substantial threat to religious liberty that this Court has never tolerated before and should not tolerate now." A bipartisan group of more than fifty national security and foreign policy officials—including those who ran the CIA, represented America at the United Nations, served as secretaries at the Departments of Defense, State, and National Security, or led White House counterterrorism efforts—filed a brief that said the ban was a "radical departure" from prior border-security policy, was not supported by any intelligence, had no credible or compelling need, actually damaged national security, and was not "deserving of this Court's deference."

One of the briefs stood out for the first name listed on it—Karen Korematsu—who along with others told the justices that they need only look to the court's own precedents "for a reminder of the constitutional costs and human suffering that flow from the Judiciary's failure to rein in sweeping governmental action against disfavored minorities."

Korematsu's father, Fred, a welder living in Oakland, California, defied a World War II–era executive order from President Franklin Delano Roosevelt in 1942 that led to the removal and incarceration of all individuals of Japanese ancestry on the entire Pacific Coast. The government sent them to barracks in desolate areas dubbed "relocation centers" that were surrounded by barbed wire and machine-gun towers. A divided Supreme Court back then ultimately sided with the government, ruling that it would not substitute its judgment for that of the military authorities when it came to wartime policies. The justices allowed the concentration camps to remain.

In the decades following the *Korematsu* decision, the country's lawmakers acknowledged the injustice of the program in a 1988 law that said it was based on "race prejudice, war hysteria, and a failure of political leadership," and among other actions offered an official apology. The Supreme Court, however, had never overturned its ruling in the case.

And now Korematsu's daughter highlighted the similarities between the government's argument in 1942 and 2018. The Trump administration was asking the court to accept the rationale offered in the proclamation and not to question whether the president showed discriminatory intent, the brief said. "Rather than repeat the failures of the past, this Court should repudiate them and affirm the greater legacy of those cases: Blind deference to the Executive Branch, even in areas in which decision-makers must wield wide discretion, is incompatible with the protection of fundamental freedoms."

But the Supreme Court already had allowed the Trump administration to implement the third version of the travel ban in December 2017, a sign that the court wasn't ready to start second-guessing the president's authority in border and national security areas.

At oral arguments in April 2018, the justices grappled with how and whether the Supreme Court should try to discern what a president is thinking when he implements a policy, and whether his motivations include religious discrimination. Justice Elena Kagan asked how the justices can analyze the adequacy of a proclamation that says important national security interests are at stake, "which for the most part we've said courts are not equipped to do." Judges have long deferred to the political branches that have the expertise and the information to make these real-world policy decisions.

Neal Katyal argued for the state of Hawaii, which sued to stop the travel ban. He urged the justices to look to what a reasonable, objective observer would conclude when looking at the travel ban. "And the best evidence of this, about what a reasonable, objective observer would think, is to look at the wide variety of amicus briefs in this case from every corner of society representing millions and millions of people," Katyal said, "from the U.S.

Conference of Catholic Bishops, which calls it 'blatant religious discrimination.'"

Justice Anthony M. Kennedy seized on a statement from Katyal to make a point about the role of the court. Katyal had just told the justices that a president has robust authority to deal with a severe threat of infiltration of the United States by terrorists. "And your argument is that courts have the duty to review whether or not there is such a national contingency; that's for the courts to do, not the president?" Kennedy asked.

Chief Justice John G. Roberts Jr. asked about how Trump could clear away claims of bias against Muslims. If the president disavowed all his previous statements that showed some bias against Muslims, and then reentered the same proclamation the next day, would that kill off the legal challenges based on discrimination against Muslims? Yes, Katyal conceded, but "the president didn't do that."

Justice Samuel A. Alito Jr. questioned whether any reasonable observer would look at the proclamation without Trump's tweets and outside statements and think it was a Muslim ban. Only five of the fifty predominantly Muslim countries are in the ban, Alito pointed out, and those account for only about 8 percent of the world's Muslim population. Katyal responded by urging the judges to look at all the circumstances around the proclamation.

Alito insisted: "My only point is that if you look at what was done, it does not look at all like a Muslim ban. There are other justifications that jump out as to why these particular countries were put on the list. So it seems to me the list creates a strong inference that this was not done for that invidious purpose."

Trump's tweets and other statements, and how much the justices would consider them, would become the heart of the case.

The court announced its decision near the end of June and split 5–4 along ideological lines, with the conservative wing voting to allow the government to keep the ban in place. Roberts, as the chief justice, assigned himself the majority opinion. It included numerous lines that indicated that while the court was ruling for the president, this shouldn't be interpreted as an endorsement of the president's Muslim comments or the travel ban itself.

"We express no view on the soundness of the policy," Roberts wrote. He noted that presidents have used their extraordinary power to speak on behalf of fellow citizens and "espouse the principles of religious freedom and tolerance on which this Nation was founded." He quoted George W. Bush's words about Islam, and America's shared values "of respect and dignity and human worth," delivered in the days after the September 11, 2001, terrorist attacks. Presidents have "performed unevenly in living up to those inspiring words," Roberts said.

But there was a big "but" coming next, and Roberts used it to describe why the court must set aside Trump's uninspiring words and judge the case based on the role of the president in the constitution. The president has great power when it comes to the country's borders and national security. The win doesn't go to Trump, in other words. It goes to the presidency.

"But the issue before us is not whether to denounce the statements. It is instead the significance of those statements in reviewing a Presidential directive, neutral on its face, addressing a matter within the core of executive responsibility," Roberts wrote. "In doing so, we must consider not only the statements of a particular President, but also the authority of the Presidency itself."

That authority means the Supreme Court is "highly constrained" from substituting its assessment for the judgments of a president. Because of that, the Supreme Court ruling appears to give Trump and future presidents great leeway in border and national security issues. Federal judges can look at a president's tweets and other statements, the majority opinion states, but they can block only a policy that has no relationship to a legitimate government interest or that is driven only by animus.

With the travel ban, the government had an interest in screening for dangerous people entering the country, and the proclamation itself says nothing about religion, Roberts wrote. And "because there is persuasive evidence that the entry suspension has a legitimate grounding in national security concerns, quite apart from any religious hostility, we must accept that independent justification."

Justice Sonia Sotomayor was not ready to accept Trump's justification, in a dissent that showed just how deeply the court divided in the case. She wrote that Trump shouldn't be able to keep a policy first advertised as a Muslim ban just because "the policy now masquerades behind a façade of national-security concerns." The justice, who often speaks about how her experiences shape her views, read a version of her scathing dissent from the bench, usually thought to be reserved for when a dissenting judge really means it.

Sotomayor called the majority's view a "watered-down legal standard" and instead adopted Katyal's suggestion of deciding what a "reasonable observer" might think. To make her point, she dedicated almost a quarter of the pages in her dissent to recounting Trump's statements about Muslims and the travel ban policy, and noted that "a reasonable observer" would conclude the ban was motivated by anti-Muslim hostility. "Given the overwhelming record evidence of anti-Muslim animus, it simply cannot be said that the Proclamation has a legitimate basis," she wrote.

Sotomayor also called out the five justices in the majority for ignoring Trump's statements about religion when, in the *Masterpiece Cakeshop* case decided just weeks earlier, they had used the anti-religion comments of a member of the Colorado Civil Rights Commission to throw out a decision against a baker who declined to make a cake for a same-sex wedding. "In both instances," she wrote, "the question is whether a government actor exhibited tolerance and neutrality in reaching a decision that affects individuals' fundamental religious freedom."

Sotomayor went on to write that the majority's decision was more troubling because of the "stark parallels" between the reasoning of the majority and *Korematsu*, the 1942 case about Japanese internment camps. The majority deployed the same dangerous logic underlying *Korematsu* when it blindly accepted the government's misguided invitation to sanction a discriminatory policy motivated by animosity toward a disfavored group in the name of a superficial claim of national security, she said.

Roberts used the majority opinion to parry the attack. It was a comparison that Roberts declared to be "wholly inapt," and he dismissed it as an effort of critics to seek a "rhetorical advantage." The forcible relocation of U.S. citizens to concentration camps is objectively unlawful,

Roberts wrote, and not at all like a facially neutral policy denying certain foreign nationals the privilege of admission.

But Roberts used the opening to do some repair work on the Supreme Court's reputation. He wrote to "express what is already obvious": that *Korematsu* was gravely wrong, has been overruled in the court of history, and has no place in law under the Constitution.

Trump responded to the decision with, of course, a tweet: "SUPREME COURT UPHOLDS TRUMP TRAVEL BAN. Wow!" He followed up by declaring that the decision was "a tremendous victory for the American people and for our Constitution."

In many ways, the victory for the Trump administration was not so tremendous. The third version of the policy was a far cry from his campaign promise of a "total and complete shutdown of Muslims." Between the lower courts and the Supreme Court, the judiciary had forced the administration to draw up a much more restrained policy. In that way, the federal courts showed that they can alter a president's actions, even as the Supreme Court defers to the president's power.

A major question remains open: did the Supreme Court basically give a roadmap to Trump and future presidents who want the court to approve discriminatory changes to the nation's borders, showing that they can do so as long as they frame it as a legitimate government interest? The justices could face similar issues again as Trump's tough-on-immigration policies spark lawsuits across the country, especially regarding the separation of migrant families on the U.S.-Mexico border.

This concern was enough to prompt Kennedy to write separately in the case "to make this further observation" that would seem to be directed at an audience of one: President Trump.

> There are numerous instances in which the statements and actions of Government officials are not subject to judicial scrutiny or intervention. That does not mean those officials are free to disregard the Constitution and the rights it proclaims and protects. The oath that all officials take to adhere to the Constitution is not confined to those spheres in which the Judiciary can correct or even comment upon what those officials say or do. Indeed, the very fact that an official may have broad discretion, discretion free from judicial scrutiny, makes it all the more imperative for him or her to adhere to the Constitution and its meaning.
>
> The First Amendment prohibits the establishment of religion and promises the free exercise of religion. From these safeguards, and from the guarantee of freedom of speech, it follows there is freedom of belief and expression. It is an urgent necessity that officials adhere to these constitutional guarantees and mandates in all their actions, even in the sphere of foreign affairs. An anxious world must know that our Government remains committed always to the liberties the Constitution seeks to preserve and protect, so that freedom extends outward, and lasts.

It was the kind of soaring and aspirational language Kennedy often used in his opinions, but here it was deployed to sound notes of resignation that the court, and he himself in turn, must defer to the president when it comes to the country's national security.

These were the final words Kennedy would write in contributing to an opinion as a Supreme Court justice.

Chapter 6

Gorsuch's Arrival

Justice Neil Gorsuch quickly established himself as a reliably conservative vote when he joined the court. He arrived for the last two months of the 2016 October Term, when there were only seventeen relatively minor cases left before the term ended in June 2017. In all those cases, Gorsuch voted with the court's most conservative justice, Clarence Thomas. He also agreed with Thomas in some of the court's decisions about which cases to hear in the future. Helgi Walker, a former Thomas clerk, dubbed the Thomas-Gorsuch union a "budding bromance."

But Gorsuch began in earnest to distinguish his own style throughout his first full term on the court, the 2017 October Term, through his questions at oral arguments, his writing, and his public appearances. His skill at writing opinions appears ready to give him sway in the conservative wing of the court, but he also showed he will not hesitate to strike out and write separately in a case to present his own view.

President Donald Trump had picked Gorsuch to be in the mold of the conservative justice whose seat he would fill, the late Antonin Scalia, and Gorsuch certainly fulfilled those Republican hopes. But during the 2017 October Term, Gorsuch disagreed with Thomas; voted opposite of the justice for whom he once clerked, Anthony M. Kennedy; and sometimes wrote detailed descriptions of the thought process behind his decisions. There were times when he appeared to annoy other justices with questions at oral argument.

So there was plenty in Gorsuch's first full term to suggest that he will spend the next decades living up to what he told the Senate Judiciary Committee during his confirmation hearings: "I am a judge, I am my own man."

The reason Gorsuch was even on the court—the pitched political battle about which president would fill the vacancy left by Scalia's death in February 2016—also gave him a big role on some consequential cases. That confirmation fight left the court shorthanded at eight justices for more than a year. During that time, the court kept a low profile and tried to avoid hearing divisive cases, since that would risk a 4–4 tie. When Gorsuch joined the bench, the court once again filled its schedule with major cases, as well as those it had been unable to decide while shorthanded.

The court had apparently deadlocked 4–4 on a case about immigration detention, *Sessions v. Dimaya,* since the justices did not issue a ruling. They agreed to rehear the case once Gorsuch was on the court. That set up Gorsuch to be the tiebreaker on an issue that was one of the main priorities of the tough-on-immigration president who appointed him, and gave the newest justice one of his best avenues to distinguish himself in his first year.

The dispute was about a lawful permanent resident from the Philippines who faced deportation because of a residential burglary, a decision that hinged on whether that crime should be interpreted as a "crime of violence" under immigration law. The U.S. Court of Appeals for the Ninth Circuit had struck down the provision that allowed people to be deported if they committed a "crime of violence" because it was too vague. The law didn't provide a clear notice of what sort of crime would trigger deportation proceedings, the Ninth Circuit ruled, and that lack of clear notice violated the Due Process Clause of the Constitution.

The case prompted Gorsuch, for his first time, to be the lone conservative to side with the court's liberals in a 5–4 opinion. The court upheld the ruling in favor of the man from the Philippines. In doing so, Gorsuch showed that he was sometimes willing to join the liberal wing to form the majority—something conservative Justice Samuel A. Alito Jr. has yet to do in twelve years on the court, according to Adam Feldman, a postdoctoral fellow at Columbia Law School and creator of a high court statistics blog, *Empirical SCOTUS*.

And it was a telling move for other reasons: Gorsuch showed he was willing to rule against the government's approach to deportation under immigration law, cutting against Trump's stances. The Department of Homeland security said the ruling "significantly undermines DHS's efforts to remove aliens convicted of certain violent crimes, including sexual assault, kidnapping, and burglary, from the United States." Gorsuch wrote a separate concurrence in *Dimaya* and spent pages quarreling with Thomas over the correct way to interpret what the nation's founders thought Due Process rights were. Gorsuch showed he was unafraid to take on the court's second-longest-serving justice on constitutional interpretation.

The concurrence also underscored how closely his view of the court's role aligns with the view of his predecessor, Scalia. Gorsuch might have reached the same ultimate result as the justices in the liberal wing, but he did so for different reasons. He based his vote squarely on a Supreme Court decision that Scalia authored in 2015, *Johnson v. United States,* which struck down similar provisions in a federal criminal law. Scalia's *Johnson* majority opinion was also joined by the liberal wing of the court, as well as Chief Justice John G. Roberts Jr. Gorsuch wrote in *Dimaya* that in both cases, judges were left to guess about whether a specific crime would qualify for the extra penalties associated with a "crime of violence." "*Johnson* held that a law that asks so much of courts while offering them so little by way of guidance is unconstitutionally vague," Gorsuch wrote. "And I do not see how we might reach a different judgment here." He had stayed true to Scalia's approach.

Dimaya also provided a taste of Gorsuch's sometimes dramatic writing style—and his approach to striking down federal laws—as he elaborated on how vague laws can cede too much power to judges and prosecutors:

> The implacable fact is that this isn't your everyday ambiguous statute. It leaves the people to guess about what the law demands—and leaves judges to make it up. You cannot discern answers to any of the questions this law begets by resorting to the traditional canons of statutory interpretation. No amount of staring at the statute's text, structure, or history will yield a clue. Nor does the statute call for the application of some preexisting body of law familiar to the judicial power.

The statute doesn't even ask for application of common experience. Choice, pure and raw, is required. Will, not judgment, dictates the result.

Gorsuch's writing ability might be what led the chief justice to assign so many 5–4 opinions to the newest member of the court. Roberts, when he is in the majority, can decide who writes the opinion. The reasons for that decision are not public. The author of a 5–4 opinion gets the best chance to shape what the court ultimately says on the most controversial issues. The assignment is less critical in a unanimous case but becomes important in a 5–4 case because it must be written in a way that doesn't prompt other justices to switch their votes. Such a switch could turn the majority opinion into a dissent. Roberts assigned Gorsuch to write five of these 5–4 decisions during the term, more than any other justice was assigned.

Several of those opinions were on politically dull cases such as the taxability of employee stock options under the Railroad Retirement Tax Act of 1937. But one of those opinions, *Epic Systems v. Lewis,* was a major workers' rights case about arbitration clauses with huge political ramifications and much at stake for the business community. The Trump administration argued that the businesses should win, reversing the stance that the Obama administration had taken in the case. The U.S. Chamber of Commerce weighed in on the side of businesses. Unions and Democratic lawmakers, meanwhile, feared a pro-business decision would put up huge barriers for workers with minimum wage and overtime disputes.

Gorsuch, writing for the court's five conservatives in the majority, ruled that arbitration clauses in employment contracts can stop workers from pursuing class-action lawsuits in those types of disputes. That would have a big effect on about 25 million workers nationwide who have such clauses in their contracts. Class-actions allow them to pool their resources and hire a lawyer to take their case, which is critical because often the disputed amount of overtime for one employee would alone be insufficient to cover a lawyer's fees for pursuing a lawsuit.

Gorsuch leaned on his view that the courts should stick to interpreting the text of the law and refrain from deciding cases based on policy preferences. He wrote that Congress, in a 1925 law, instructed federal courts to enforce arbitration agreements according to their own terms, and that those terms can require individual—and not class—proceedings. "This Court is not free to substitute its preferred economic policies for those chosen by the people's representatives," Gorsuch wrote. "The policy may be debatable but the law is clear: Congress has instructed that arbitration agreements like those before us must be enforced as written."

The four liberal justices thought that view ignored the text and history of federal laws, but they came up one vote short. Justice Ruth Bader Ginsburg, writing a dissent, called Gorsuch's majority opinion "egregiously wrong" and suggested Congress pass a law to allow workers to act in concert, saying it "is urgently in order."

Labor unions and workers' rights groups used the opinion to point out that the decision was a political one from a Trump appointee. The Constitutional Accountability Center, which filed a brief in the case siding with workers, said conservative interest groups who lobbied and spent millions to see Gorsuch confirmed wanted him to be "a legal vending machine" once he got to the bench. "Justice Gorsuch's opinion today in *Epic* has only validated that," Elizabeth Wydra, the group's president, said.

Democratic lawmakers also criticized Gorsuch and the conservative majority for benefiting big Republican corporate interests. Representative Jerrold Nadler of New York, the top Democrat on the House Judiciary Committee, said the ruling meant "the conservative wing of the Court has now warped arbitration into a cudgel against hardworking Americans that deprives them of the right to seek collective relief."

Gorsuch also set himself apart from the tough-on-crime conservative justices in several cases, parting ways with Thomas and Alito. Gorsuch sided with liberals in a 6–3 decision in *Class v. United States* to let a criminal defendant appeal his conviction. He also did so in 7–2 and 6–3 decisions siding with defendants in sentencing disputes, *Rosales-Mireles v. United States* and *Hughes v. United States,* respectively. He joined the liberal wing in a 7–2 decision holding that prosecutors had not sufficiently proved obstruction of justice in a criminal tax law case, *Marinello v. United States.* Gorsuch did not write separately in any of those cases to explain his individual views.

But Gorsuch struck a tough-on-crime tone in the case of a Georgia man appealing his death sentence, *Wilson v. Sellers.* The Supreme Court's decision in the case gave federal courts—if they were reviewing a state court ruling that had upheld a prisoner's death sentence without stating the reasons why it was doing so—permission to dig into previous rulings in the case to find the reasons. Gorsuch wrote the dissent in that 6–3 case, arguing that the federal law does not allow for such judicial freelancing.

Gorsuch would go on to disappoint Democrats and their allies for the rest of the term, even when he wasn't writing the majority opinion. In *Masterpiece Cakeshop,* Gorsuch used his concurrence to tangle with Justice Elena Kagan about how to assess claims from companies that do not want to make cakes for same-sex weddings, casting himself as the leading conservative voice when the Supreme Court gets another case that pits religious freedom against anti-discrimination laws.

There were no real surprises in his decisions.

Gorsuch's writing and behavior on the bench did not escape the microscope of the media. He was in the middle of the pack when it came to the number of questions asked from his perch on the right side of the bench, but many of his statements to the attorneys came across as trying too hard. In the partisan gerrymandering case he came across as a bit condescending in comments to Paul Smith, one of the nation's most experienced appellate lawyers: "For that matter, maybe we can just for a second talk about the arcane matter, the Constitution," Gorsuch told Smith.

Gorsuch then pondered aloud where the Supreme Court got the power to tell state lawmakers how to draw their congressional districts. Smith, who has handled appeals on that very issue, said there was nothing unusual about it, and "that's what the court has been doing." At that point, Ginsburg jumped in with a question about the Supreme Court's precedents in the area, aimed at Gorsuch. "Where did one-person/one-vote come from?" Ginsburg asked.

Some press reports jumped on the drama. Jeffrey Toobin of *The New Yorker* called Ginsburg's comments a "slap."

Around the same time, veteran Supreme Court reporter Joan Biskupic of CNN reported that word seeped out—via clerks and other staff, through the justices' friends, and through the justices themselves—that Gorsuch had strained relationships between the justices. "Such communications make clear that Gorsuch has generated some ill will among justices," Biskupic wrote. "Signs have emerged from the bench, too, as Gorsuch has been on the receiving end of a few retorts."

Kagan, at a public appearance, rejected the idea that the justices weren't getting along. And Thomas, who rarely does television interviews, went on Fox News and disputed the reports. "He is a good man and I have no idea what they are talking about," Thomas said.

Gorsuch had a reputation as a good writer from his time on the U.S. Court of Appeals for the Tenth Circuit, but his first dissent of the term in a procedural case also generated some parody of his writing style among law professors. Gorsuch's sin in their eyes was starting with the English writer and philosopher G. K. Chesterton: "Chesterton reminds us not to clear away a fence just because we cannot see its point," Gorsuch wrote. "Even if a fence doesn't seem to have a reason, sometimes all that means is we need to look more carefully for the reason it was built in the first place."

Some mocking of the line on Twitter prompted *The New York Times* to ask, "Is His Writing Really All That Bad?" Nina Varsava, a law student and doctoral candidate in literature, analyzed his writing from the Tenth Circuit and told the *Times* she found it held up "exceedingly well." But she said that his Supreme Court opinions felt more heavy-handed, "a little contrived, a little too much."

Almost all of the chatter about his writing and behind-the-scenes relationships with other justices had faded by the end of the term.

Gorsuch did not shy away from political events. In September, less than two weeks before the start of the term, Gorsuch traveled to Kentucky to speak at the University of Louisville. There to introduce Gorsuch was Kentucky Republican Senator Mitch McConnell, who as majority leader made the highly controversial and historic move to block Obama's pick to the court and held open the seat for Trump to fill. McConnell then changed Senate rules to prevent Democrats from being able to block Gorsuch's confirmation vote. The *Lexington Herald-Leader* covered Gorsuch's speech, including lines about how judges are not political. "I don't believe in red judges or blue judges," Gorsuch said, echoing a similar line from his confirmation hearing. "We wear black." Seated behind him, McConnell smiled at the line, the paper reported.

A week later, Gorsuch gave a speech to a conservative group at Trump International Hotel in Washington, D.C. While he reportedly stayed away from politics in his comments, the fact that the speech took place at the hotel of a president whose administration had cases before the court brought protesters outside and criticism from the left. "Justice Gorsuch speaking to a conservative group in the Trump Hotel, where the President continues to hold a financial stake, is everything that was wrong with his nomination," Senate Minority Leader Charles E. Schumer of New York said in a news release. "There's a reason we questioned his independence during his confirmation hearings."

And in November, Gorsuch addressed a black-tie gathering in Washington, D.C. of The Federalist Society, a group of conservative lawyers that played a role in his selection and confirmation. Gorsuch cracked jokes about not getting along with his colleagues, and about criticism of his style of questioning from the bench. But mostly he used the occasion to repeat how he would stick to his conservative approach to deciding cases, and promised to be on the court for a very long time.

In January, Gorusch attended Trump's State of the Union Address. It is one of the few times the nation gets to see the justices on television. The speech has been the scene of politics before, most notably in 2010 when Alito mouthed "not true" when Obama criticized the Supreme Court's decision in a campaign finance case. Alito has avoided the address since then, and Thomas does not attend either. Gorsuch was very aware that he would be under the microscope. When Trump mentioned Gorsuch's appointment as one of the major accomplishments of his presidency to date, the television cameras cut to shots of Gorsuch. He sat frozen with a steely gaze, not moving a muscle except to blink.

Gorsuch might have brought his poker face for that moment, not wanting to betray an air of neutrality. But McConnell and Trump would not be so restrained at the end of the term, when Gorsuch would help deliver a string of conservative victories on major social and political issues.

The Sword of Free Speech

The Supreme Court had only one major opinion to reveal on the last day of the term in June 2018, but there was a lack of the familiar buzz around the courthouse about which way the ruling would go. Typically, the end of the term is pregnant with drama because the justices reveal decisions in the most high-profile and controversial cases just before a three-month summer break. The cases left for last are usually the most hotly contested between the justices, so they are more likely to fret over every word. They are more likely to send drafts back and forth between chambers, trying to convince other justices to join their side. The dissents are more likely to be passionate—and all of these things take time and push the court right up against the deadline.

But on this last day of the 2017 October Term, court watchers knew it was highly likely that the Supreme Court would deal a major financial blow to Democratic candidates. In the end, it would be at the hand of conservative Justice Samuel A. Alito Jr., who might have had a version of such a decision tucked away in a drawer and ready to go for years. The opinion in *Janus v. American Federation of State County and Municipal Employees* would come out 5–4, with the conservative justices outnumbering the liberal justices. And it meant unions that represent teachers and other public-sector workers would no longer be able to collect fees from employees who don't want to be members.

The decision came down at 10:02 a.m. President Donald Trump took to Twitter nine minutes later to gloat: "Supreme Court rules in favor of non-union workers who are now, as an example, able to support a candidate of his or her choice without having those who control the Union deciding for them. Big loss for the coffers of the Democrats!"

It was the fifth time Trump would cheer a Supreme Court decision in the last month of the term, a sign of just how much his election, and his subsequent appointment of Justice Neil Gorsuch, had given a lasting conservative tilt to the court and the nation's legal landscape.

Not only did Gorsuch provide a crucial fifth vote in the thirteen decisions during the term that split the court 5–4 along its familiar ideological lines, but he sided with the Trump administration in a number of highly political cases that advanced the policy agenda of conservatives.

Democrats and their political allies had held out hope of big victories during the term in two areas: ending partisan gerrymandering and defending LGBT rights related to same-sex weddings. But Justice Anthony M. Kennedy, the conservative who seemed open to joining the court's liberal wing on those issues, dashed those hopes earlier in the term. He did not swing to the liberal side in any 5–4 case this term, making it one of his most conservative runs in years.

As a result, the 2017 October Term illustrates the type of decisions the court could produce if Trump successfully appoints another reliable conservative to the court to replace Kennedy—especially in cases that feature the First Amendment and turn on whether the government can compel a person to speak.

The ruling on the final day in the union case highlights the vast sway the Supreme Court can have in the political world if the majority asserts itself—and the risk to its reputation for doing so. The only question in the *Janus* case was whether the justices should overturn the court's 1977 ruling in *Abood v. Detroit Board of Education.* The *Abood* decision had allowed unions to collect "agency fees" from teachers and other public-sector employees who are not members. Those fees strengthened unions by letting them avoid "free-riders," or nonmembers who would enjoy the benefits of a union's work, such as collective bargaining with the state to raise salaries, without contributing any dues.

While the agency fees could not be used for the union's political activities, the ability to collect them helped keep the unions financially stable. Union dues historically have helped fuel the campaigns of Democrats who support workers' rights, as opposed to Republicans who tend to back business interests. Public-sector unions, of which the American Federation of State, County, and Municipal Employees (AFSCME) is one, contributed $60 million to Democrats during the 2016 campaign, compared to just $8 million to Republicans, according to statistics from the Center for Responsive Politics.

Big political money also went into years of legal efforts to strike down the forty-one–year-old ruling in *Abood.* The parent organization of the National Right to Work Legal Defense Foundation, which has represented workers challenging the agency fees in several high-profile case, has spent more than $10 million lobbying Congress on union issues since 2012, according to a Senate database of lobbying disclosure records. The parent group's funding has been linked to organizations associated with Republican megadonors Charles and David Koch, such as Freedom Partners Chamber of Commerce, which gave $1 million in 2012, according to the Center for Responsive Politics.

Alito and the conservative wing of the court had expressed an openness to overruling *Abood* in a series of cases going back to 2012. They suggested that the ruling violated the First Amendment rights of nonmembers who disagreed with the union's actions but were compelled to fund them. In those cases, Justice Elena Kagan and the liberal wing countered that there were no special legal justifications for reversing *Abood*. But the conservative wing showed no signs of hesitating in the *Janus* case.

Ahead of the arguments in February 2018, Senate Majority Leader Mitch McConnell, R-Ky., told *The New York Times* that a ruling against unions could have an impact on Democratic fundraising. He described the *Janus* case as "an example" of why he found it important to block President Barack Obama from filling the vacancy left by the death of the conservative Justice Antonin Scalia. The thirty-three–year veteran of the Senate told the *Kentucky Today* editorial board in April that the move, which allowed Trump to nominate Gorsuch, "was the most consequential decision I've made in my entire public career."

On the other side of the political aisle, Democrats reminded the justices to think about the court's standing in the eyes of the American public. Senators Sheldon White-house of Rhode Island and Richard Blumenthal of Connecticut, members of the Judiciary Committee and former attorneys general of their states, filed a brief in the case to urge the justices to respect precedent and leave *Abood* alone. If the justices overturned *Abood,* the duo wrote, the Supreme Court would "face growing skepticism about its ability to carry out its constitutional responsibilities in an apolitical manner."

The senators warned that the *Janus* case was brought by "sophisticated and powerful interests" that "appear in droves to enlist federal courts as their agents in political contests." A precedent should not be overturned after decades simply because there are different justices on the court, the senators warned, or the court's "decision-making begins to look like prize-taking."

In a plea directed specifically to Chief Justice John G. Roberts Jr., the senators brought up the concern he raised during oral argument in the partisan gerrymandering case. Roberts had asked in *Gill* about what the "intelligent man on the street" would think of the court's "status and integrity" if it were to continually adjudicate political disputes. Heed that warning in this case as well, the senators said: "Otherwise, the 'intelligent man' will reach only one conclusion: that the Court is being asked to reach a political decision because the interests involved in that campaign think—and have telegraphed and telegraphed and telegraphed—that, based on this Court's changed membership, a 5-4 victory awaits them."

Alito and the conservatives had done everything they could to telegraph what they wanted to do with the *Abood* case. Back during his confirmation in 2006, the U.S. Chamber of Commerce and other business interests supported Alito as a consistently conservative appeals court judge. After he joined the court, Alito and Roberts ranked first and second in a study of how pro-business justices had voted since 1946, according to a *Minnesota Law Review* study from 2013. The study concluded the pair had helped make the court "highly" pro-business. Compared to previous eras, the court under Roberts takes more cases in which the business litigant lost in the lower court and then reverses the lower court's decision.

But ending *Abood* would be a six-year process. Alito started the effort back in 2012, when he wrote the majority opinion in *Knox v. SEIU*. The decision prevented the union from forcing nonmember employees to pay more agency fees when the union wanted more money to lobby against a state ballot proposition. Alito used that opinion to argue the broader point. He wrote that policies meant to curtail free-riders "are generally insufficient to overcome First Amendment objections" because they force nonmembers to subsidize speech they might disagree with. Alito wrote that *Abood* and another previous case "approach, if they do not cross, the limit of what the First Amendment can tolerate." Justices Roberts, Scalia, Kennedy, and Thomas all signed on to that view.

Justice Sonia Sotomayor, joined by Justice Ruth Bader Ginsburg, had agreed with the ruling in *Knox* but took exception to how Alito went out of his way to have the court cast doubt on its own *Abood* decision, "on our own invitation and without adversarial presentation." The task of courts is to answer constitutional questions, Sotomayor wrote, but the majority "today decides to ask them as well."

Less than a year later, the National Right to Work Legal Defense Foundation would bring the court a case that asked the question that Alito had posed in *Knox*. Alito also wrote the 5–4 majority decision in that 2014 case, *Harris v. Quinn*. In it, the court ruled that the First Amendment prohibited agency fees for home health care workers who were partial public-sector employees. While the majority opinion again questioned the *Abood* decision, calling it "questionable on several grounds," the court said *Abood* applied only to full public-sector employees and so could not be part of this case. That detail kept Alito and the conservatives from overturning *Abood* at that time.

The next year, in 2015, the Supreme Court agreed to hear *Friedrichs v. California Teachers Association,* a case that directly asked them to overturn *Abood*. The oral argument in January 2016 made it clear the court had the votes to do so. But Scalia died during a hunting trip to Texas in February, before the justices could rule. Over in the Senate, McConnell had immediately announced that there would be no confirmation vote on any Obama pick to fill the seat. The shorthanded court was equally divided 4–4 in the case, a deadlock that meant the lower court ruling would be upheld. The *Abood* precedent escaped once again unscathed.

Abood would not be so fortunate in 2018. The newest challenge featured Mark Janus, a child-support specialist at the Illinois Department of Healthcare and Family Services who refused to join the union because he opposes many of the public policy positions it advocates during collective bargaining. The National Right to Work Legal Defense Foundation represented Janus, who did not want to pay

an agency fee of $44.58 per month. The dollar amount for
Janus might be low, but it finally gave Alito the votes and
the right case to plunge the knife into *Abood*.

First, Alito wrote for the majority that *Abood* was
wrong to justify agency fees, because the risk of free-
riders was not enough to force a nonmember to subsidize
a union's work during collective bargaining. In collective
bargaining a union can speak about controversial topics,
from compelling Illinois to appropriate $75 million to
fund a 2 percent wage increase, to "climate change, the
Confederacy, sexual orientation and gender identity, evo-
lution, and minor religions," Alito wrote.

Those controversial topics are undoubtedly matters of
concern to the public and merit special protection under
the First Amendment, he wrote. Employees can waive
those First Amendment rights only by affirmatively con-
senting to pay.

Then, Alito spent pages defending why the court
should not follow *stare decisis* and allow *Abood* to stand.
The decision was "not well reasoned," Alito concluded, it
"has proven unworkable," and it was decided "against a
very different legal and economic backdrop" of the new
phenomenon of public-sector unionism.

Moreover, the court's own fight to end *Abood* provided
an additional reason to overturn it. Public-sector unions
shouldn't have relied on *Abood*, Alito wrote, because they
"have been on notice for years regarding this Court's mis-
givings" about the precedent.

"We recognize that the loss of payments from nonmembers may cause unions to experience unpleasant transition
costs in the short term, and may require unions to make
adjustments in order to attract and retain members," Alito

wrote. "But we must weigh these disadvantages against the considerable windfall that unions have received under *Abood* for the past 41 years. It is hard to estimate how many billions of dollars have been taken from nonmembers and transferred to public-sector unions in violation of the First Amendment. Those unconstitutional exactions cannot be allowed to continue indefinitely."

Justice Elena Kagan, in an impassioned dissent joined by the liberal wing of the court, called it "judicial disruption." Rarely, if ever, had the court thrown out a precedent with so little regard for *stare decisis,* she wrote. Her conclusion: "The majority has overruled *Abood* for no exceptional or special reason, but because it never liked the decision. It has overruled *Abood* because it wanted to."

Abood was workable, Kagan wrote, and more than twenty states had laws based on it that underpinned thousands of ongoing contracts involving millions of employees. But she went beyond just the *Janus* case to reveal even more about what the liberal wing fears about how the court might use the First Amendment and compelled speech to proactively strike down laws they don't like.

"Maybe most alarming, the majority has chosen the winners by turning the First Amendment into a sword, and using it against workaday economic and regulatory policy," Kagan wrote. "Today is not the first time the Court has wielded the First Amendment in such an aggressive way. And it threatens not to be the last."

Just a day earlier, Justice Stephen Breyer had raised similar concerns when the court's conservatives had used a First Amendment argument about compelled speech to rule against a California law on the hot-button topic of abortion.

California had required licensed crisis pregnancy centers—which it said were pro-life, largely Christian belief-based organizations—to post notices to inform patients about free or low-cost abortions under state health care programs. The state's lawmakers said the purpose was to ensure that residents know their rights and the health care services available to them. The state said requiring the centers to inform patients would be the most effective way to get the information to women facing a time-sensitive pregnancy decision.

The National Institute of Family and Life Advocates and other centers with religious affiliations argued that the measure violated their First Amendment rights because it compelled them to deliver the government's message about abortion, "a subject where there is profound moral and ideological disagreement." The groups said they have a sole mission to encourage childbirth: "Forcing a pro-life group to advertise for abortion has to be unconstitutional, yet that is what California's Reproductive FACT Act does."

Like all cases that touch on abortion, *NIFLA v. Becerra* was a political lightning rod. The pregnancy centers were represented by Alliance Defending Freedom (ADF), a Christian-based group that has been involved in numerous controversial cases before the Supreme Court on abortion, contraception, same-sex marriage, and other religious issues. ADF has ties to and an ongoing working relationship with the Trump administration. The group also represented the baker in the *Masterpiece Cakeshop* case. The Trump administration brief officially stated that the government did not support either side, but it urged the court to find the California law unconstitutional when it came to pregnancy centers that were licensed by the state. A group of 144 Republican members of Congress filed a brief urging the court to strike down California's law, while a group of 100 Democratic and independent lawmakers argued the other way.

Justice Clarence Thomas, writing for the majority in the 5–4 decision, said that California can't co-opt the licensed pregnancy centers to deliver the message for the state. The disclosure requirement changed the message that the pregnancy centers delivered, from one that was strictly pro-life to one that was pro-choice. That type of law can be justified only if the government proves it has a good reason to do so, Thomas wrote.

But the more strident explanation of the issue came from Kennedy, who wrote a concurrence joined by Roberts, Alito, and Gorsuch that called the law the "paradigmatic example of the serious threat" of the government's imposing its own message on individuals. "This compels individuals to contradict their most deeply held beliefs, beliefs grounded in basic philosophical, ethical, or religious precepts, or all of these," Kennedy wrote. "Freedom of speech secures freedom of thought and belief. This law imperils those liberties."

Breyer saw some serious problems with the approach the majority took. Taken literally, Breyer wrote, it could be used to attack the validity of most government regulations. "What about laws requiring hospitals to talk about vaccines or seat belts, laws requiring landlords to tell tenants about garbage disposal rules, laws regulating securities or consumer products, laws requiring professionals, doctors, lawyers, engineers, accountants, to disclose information to their clients?" Breyer asked from the bench when he read his dissent.

Chapter 7

While the majority wrote that the ruling would not question health and safety warnings or factual and uncontroversial disclosures about commercial products, Breyer pointed out, California justified its law on health and safety considerations. The ruling would allow judges across the nation to use the First Amendment to rule on social and economic regulations, Breyer wrote in the dissent, "striking down laws that judges may disfavor, while upholding others."

On that day, however, the court had given abortion opponents a boost in the culture war. The president of NIFLA, Thomas Glessner, said the pregnancy centers were pleased with the decision "and for what it means for the many pro-life centers that serve and empower women in California and throughout the country." A vice president at the liberal Center for American Progress (CAP) said the decision would allow the centers to continue spreading "propaganda and lies" that targeted low-income women and minorities, who would suffer the most.

"By siding with fake health care centers, the Court has made public health second to far-right political views," Shilpa Phadke of CAP said. "Justice Thomas's decision appears to be an assist from the bench to the Trump administration and anti-choice politicians across the country who seek to restrict the speech of legitimate doctors while empowering fake medicine."

In the Senate, McConnell's reaction to the decision consisted of one photo his campaign tweeted just minutes after the Supreme Court released opinions in *NIFLA* as well as the travel ban case. It was a photo of the Kentucky Republican about to shake hands with Neil Gorsuch when they met on Capitol Hill during the Senate's confirmation process. Without saying a word, it underscored how McConnell's decision that created a year of drama about the Supreme Court confirmation process ultimately led to drama-free wins for Republicans—and set up more victories for his side in the future.

Chapter 8

Shifting Right

President Donald Trump took office in January 2017 and set to work reversing his predecessor's policies on climate change, gun control, trade, immigration, affirmative action, health care, oversight of Wall Street, transgender students' use of bathrooms, and even importing elephant trophies from Zimbabwe. Trump had pledged during the campaign that on his first day in the White House, he would "cancel every unconstitutional executive action, memorandum, and order issued by President Obama." His administration was just as determined when it came to reversing the Obama administration's legal strategy in Supreme Court cases ahead of the 2017 October Term.

The Justice Department boldly changed legal positions in high-profile cases in ways that lined up with Republican policy interests on voting rights, workers' rights, and social rights—moves that ultimately delivered political wins to Republicans and the Trump administration. It was enough for Justice Sonia Sotomayor to question the government's reasons for the flips during oral argument in two of the cases, and for Attorney General Jeff Sessions to crow on the last day of the term about the Trump administration's successes.

"In four cases, after careful review, we changed the Department's position in order to follow the law," Sessions said. "The favorable Supreme Court decisions in all four cases reflect that we took the proper course of action. The decisions speak for themselves." Among them, one of those cases is expected to give Republicans an advantage at the polls in future elections, and another will hurt Democratic fundraising. Even in bragging, Sessions understated the role the Trump administration's reversals played in other controversial cases.

There's no way to know for sure whether the conservative Supreme Court would have ruled differently if Democratic candidate Hillary Clinton had won the 2016 presidential election and continued on with Obama-era legal positions.

Yet the Trump administration's legal reversals highlight how political parties are increasingly turning to the courts, and to the Supreme Court in particular, to score victories in the nation's policy fights. In a country where Congress is stuck in partisan gridlock and unable to pass many laws, frustrated presidents, states, and citizens have turned to the federal court system to get their way. And if those cases all go one way—as they did in the 2017 October Term—the court opens itself up to criticism that it is just delivering partisan results.

"We appear to have reached a point where litigants appearing before the Supreme Court in certain matters can anticipate victory or defeat because of the identity of the parties, not the merits of the case," Senator Sheldon Whitehouse, a Rhode Island Democrat on the Senate Judiciary

Committee, said at the end of the term. "The predictability of these 5–4 partisan decisions by the Republican majority, and the alignment of the outcomes with the interests of the Republican donors, is a cancer on the credibility of the Court."

The Trump administration exerted its influence at the Supreme Court through an arm of the Justice Department that is powerful but not well known outside of legal circles. The U.S. Solicitor General's Office represents the federal government before the court and helps shape the legal strategy for the administration. The office is one of the court's best customers, getting involved in about two-thirds of the cases each term. The U.S. government is the prosecutor in criminal cases, the defender of federal laws, the lawyer for agencies that get sued, and an institutional voice that carries considerable weight in other cases of great national importance. Traditionally, the office looks out for the long-term interests of the federal government, not necessarily the policy positions of a particular president. The head of that office, the solicitor general, is the fourth-highest-ranking official at the Justice Department. The job is mainly a legal one. But it is also political, since the president appoints the solicitor general, and the attorney general, a member of the president's cabinet, oversees the work.

So that leaves the question: when should the solicitor general change sides in legal disputes after a new president from a different party with different policy positions and priorities is elected? Two former solicitors general were asked this question at a panel discussion for a legal group in Washington, D.C. in May 2018. One was Paul Clement, a solicitor general in the George W. Bush administration, who said any changes were really "at the margins," and that "if both administrations are looking out for the long-term interests of the executive branch, they really shouldn't change that much."

The other former solicitor general was Justice Elena Kagan, who was the first solicitor general during the Obama administration. Kagan said the lawyers who worked at the Solicitor General's Office when she took the job made it "very clear that you were supposed to think long and hard, and then you were supposed to think long and hard again, before you changed anything." That's not to say new administrations don't change directions in cases, Kagan said, but the bar should be high. "The credibility of the office in great measure depends on the idea that judges actually believe that that's what you're doing," Kagan said. "And it's the right thing to do, that's what you're there for, is to serve the long-term interests of the United States. So I think changing positions is a really big deal."

Kagan didn't mention the Trump administration, but the timing of her answer was unmistakable. Earlier that day, the Supreme Court's conservatives had sided with the Trump administration in a 5–4 decision in which the Solicitor General's Office had switched sides. In her dissent Justice Ruth Bader Ginsburg had called the majority "egregiously wrong."

The Trump administration isn't the only one to switch positions. The Obama Justice Department also switched positions in a way that prompted a rebuke from Chief Justice John G. Roberts Jr. As Josh Blackman, a professor at the South Texas College of Law in Houston who closely follows the court, wrote in an article in the *Illinois Law*

Review, "Sensing a disquieting trend, Chief Justice Roberts sent a message of sorts to the Obama administration: 'We are seeing a lot of that lately. It's perfectly fine if you want to change your position, but don't tell us it's because the secretary has reviewed the matter further, the secretary is now of the view. Tell us it's because there is a new secretary.'"

Kagan and Clement both said their time as the solicitor general was fairly free of politics, but there were some issues on which the legal policy came from the top. As Kagan put it: "There are some decisions that are just the president's to make."

With Trump, the country had a president who seemed obsessed with voting fraud and had gotten nowhere with his efforts to combat it. Yet a Supreme Court case gave his administration a chance to shape election law in a way that could help Republicans across the country. To be on the right side of the case politically, the Trump administration had to cast aside a long-held government legal position on two federal laws that were meant to boost voter registration.

The case started ahead of the 2016 presidential election in Ohio, a perennial swing state with a history of serving as a harbinger of who would win the White House. Some eligible voters showed up to the polls for a November 2015 election and were told they were no longer registered to vote. It turns out state election officials that summer had used what they call a "supplemental process" to purge voters from the registration rolls, the list of all eligible voters. Like election officials across the nation, those in Ohio want to maintain accurate rolls. Part of that effort is to make sure people who have moved, or died, or become felons are no longer listed as eligible to vote.

Republican state election officials send out more than a million cards to registered Ohio voters, asking them to confirm that they live at the same address. Voters who do not return the card—and then fail to vote in any election for four more years—are presumed to have moved and are removed from the rolls. The most important part of Ohio's process is that the cards are sent to voters who have failed to vote for two years.

A voting rights group, the A. Philip Randolph Institute, led the American Civil Liberties Union and other organizations in a challenge to that process ahead of the 2016 presidential election. The groups argued that the state's law violates federal voter-registration laws that say voters can't be removed from registration rolls simply because they didn't vote. The groups wanted the voters who had been purged—including those who had voted in the high-turnout 2008 elections but not since—to be put back on the rolls. Just because the voters didn't vote or return the card did not mean they were no longer eligible to vote, they argued.

Republicans would be helped under the supplemental policy because voters in that party are more likely to go to the polls in years when the president is not elected, an analysis from *Reuters* found. Voters were struck from the rolls in Democratic-leaning neighborhoods at roughly twice the rate as in Republican neighborhoods in the state's three largest counties, the analysis found.

The voter groups gained a powerful ally in the case when the U.S. government under the Obama administration backed the voters with a filing in July 2016. The Justice

Department explained in a brief that it had issued guidance in 2010 on this exact issue, and had expressed that view in legal actions through Republican and Democratic administrations going back to 1994. States must have reliable evidence that a voter has moved or should no longer be on the rolls and can't just remove him or her based on a voter's inactivity and then failure to return a card, the government said. A state that sends cards based solely on voter inactivity inevitably removes voters based on nonvoting, which is against the law, the government argued.

A federal appeals court agreed with the United States and the voting groups. Ohio would appeal to the Supreme Court. But before the court could weigh in, the November 2016 presidential election intervened.

Despite his win (in Ohio and the country as a whole) in that election, Trump repeatedly claimed (without proof) that there were millions of fraudulent voters that cost him the popular vote (he won the White House via the Electoral College). Trump described how voters brought in on buses from Massachusetts kept him from winning New Hampshire, and claimed that people voted many times in California, and he started a voter-fraud commission to investigate the issue nationwide. The commission later disbanded, finding no proof of widespread illegal votes. Trump responded in part by calling for laws that require voters to show a photo identification before they can cast a ballot.

Trump's call for more secure elections dovetails with broader Republican efforts in many parts of the country to pass bills with the stated purpose of combating election fraud. Voter rights groups have responded by pointing to the lack of proof of widespread illegal voting and by arguing that these laws are tailored to suppress votes from the types of citizens who historically vote for Democrats, especially black and Hispanic voters. "Ohio's method of purging the voter rolls must be viewed in the broader context of state and local efforts to make it increasingly difficult for minority voters to register to vote," Samuel Spital, a litigator at the NAACP Legal Defense and Educational Fund, said.

The Supreme Court had boosted those efforts in its 2013 ruling, *Shelby County v. Holder*. In a 5–4 decision, with the conservative wing in the majority, the justices struck down a key enforcement mechanism in the Voting Rights Act of 1965 that let the Justice Department stop discriminatory voting laws in some states before they went into effect. Chief Justice John G. Roberts Jr., writing the opinion, said that the provision was out of date, that "our country has changed," and he urged Congress to update the law to make it constitutional. Although the Voting Rights Act had been reauthorized in 2006 overwhelmingly in the House and unanimously in the Senate, and signed into law by a Republican, President George W. Bush, Republicans in Congress showed no interest in restoring the federal civil rights law. Republican lawmakers in North Carolina wasted no time in passing a law in 2013 with provisions—a strict voter ID requirement, reduction of early voting, and more—that an appeals court would later conclude targeted black voters "with almost surgical precision."

The Supreme Court in May 2017 agreed to hear the Ohio case, *Husted v. A. Philip Randolph Institute*. Three months later, the Trump administration filed a brief that cast aside the government's long-held legal position and sided with Ohio officials. The government simply said it had "reconsidered the question" after the "change in Administration" and concluded that the law does not prohibit states from using nonvoting to start the process of purging voter rolls.

Congress had passed the voter registration laws in 1993 to "increase the number of eligible citizens who register to vote," the solicitor general's brief stated, but Congress also recognized that accurate registration lists are essential to preventing voter fraud.

The Trump administration's move prompted a group of former Justice Department officials, including Obama's attorney general Eric H. Holder Jr., to file a brief to inform the justices of the department's previous, long-argued view that had been successful in lower courts. And the officials highlighted how career lawyers at the department who enforce voter registration laws had not signed the Trump administration's brief—a sign of great discord between the new administration and the department.

The NAACP Legal Defense and Educational Fund also pointed out to the justices in a brief that the Justice Department's "about-face" came without any principled explanation of its new position, such as new insights or understandings or emerging studies. The group urged the court to withhold the respect the justices usually give the Justice Department, since that respect "is based on the premise that the Department will represent the public interest, not simply parrot the ideological views of a new Administration."

In January 2018, during oral argument on the case, Justice Sonia Sotomayor asked the solicitor general, Noel Francisco, to explain why he thought that many presidents and more than forty states were interpreting the law incorrectly. "Seems quite unusual that your office would change its position so dramatically," Sotomayor said. "Do you believe this doesn't have an impact, a negative impact on certain groups in this society?"

Francisco responded that there was nothing in the law to prevent states from using nonvoting as a trigger to start the process of removing a voter from the registration rolls. It reflects the balance Congress tried to strike between "on the one hand, dramatically increasing the number of voters on the voter rolls but, on the other, giving states the flexibility they need to manage the issues that arise when you have overinflated voter rolls," Francisco said.

Sotomayor also said there was a strong case that the Ohio program is discriminatory. But Eric Murphy, the Ohio official arguing the case, pointed out that the impact of the law was not at issue. The voter groups brought the case only on the legal theory that the federal law prevented the Ohio purge program, and did not include allegations that it was discriminatory.

The Supreme Court sided with Ohio in the case, in another 5–4 decision along ideological lines. Justice Samuel A. Alito Jr., writing for the majority, pointed to the scope of the problem facing elections officials. An estimated 24 million voter registrations in the United States are either invalid or significantly inaccurate, which amounts to about one in eight voters. He wrote that Ohio's method for clearing those from the rolls is not based solely on someone's record of not voting—it's also based on their not returning the card from the state. And he highlighted how the law points to such a notice as one solution to the problem of voters being inappropriately stricken from the voter rolls. "It was Congress's judgment that a reasonable person with an interest in voting is not likely to ignore notice of this sort," Alito wrote. "We have no authority to second-guess Congress or to decide whether Ohio's Supplemental Process is the ideal method for keeping its voting rolls up to date."

Justice Stephen G. Breyer, in a dissent joined by the court's liberal wing, wrote that the nonreturned card doesn't tell state election officials anything other than that the person didn't return the card. Breyer pointed out that about 13 percent of the state's voting population did not send back their cards, and yet "the streets of Ohio's cities are not filled with moving vans." Sotomayor filed a passionate dissent of her own, less focused on the details of the Ohio law and more on the broader context of the decision in the history of the country. She accused the conservatives in the majority of entirely ignoring the history of voter suppression and upholding "a program that appears to further the very disenfranchisement of minority and low-income voters that Congress set out to eradicate."

At the time of the Supreme Court's decision, five states had similar laws: Georgia, Oklahoma, Oregon, Pennsylvania, and West Virginia. But activists such as Judith Browne Dianis, a civil rights lawyer and executive director of the Advancement Project, fear the *Husted* decision could pave the way for other states to adopt similar laws to purge voter rolls. The decision is alarming in its adoption of antivoter rhetoric, Dianis told the Congressional Black Caucus, a group of black federal lawmakers.

The decision offers "a quasi-endorsement of the more aggressive voter purge systems in places like South Carolina that could extend to states that have similar removal procedures to Ohio's, places like Wisconsin, Pennsylvania,

Georgia, states that are, unsurprisingly, key electoral players," Dianis said.

Trump tweeted about the *Husted* decision the morning it was announced: "Just won big Supreme Court decision on Voting! Great News!"

The wins kept coming for the Trump administration in cases in which it flipped positions. The Obama administration at an appeals court in Washington, D.C. had defended the appointment of judges inside the Securities and Exchange Commission who enforced investor laws. But at the Supreme Court, the Trump administration sided with a former investment advisor who brought the challenge against the commission. In *Lucia v. SEC,* the Supreme Court ruled 7–2 for the investment advisor in the case.

In *Janus,* the public-sector union case, the Trump administration detailed why it felt the argument the Obama administration had made on the same issue was wrong. Sotomayor once again made a point of asking about the change during oral arguments. "By the way, how many times this term already have you flipped positions from prior administrations?" Sotomayor asked. At that point in the term, the answer was three.

But not every decision to reverse longstanding Justice Department positions had to do with just the case at hand—for example, the *Masterpiece Cakeshop* case about same-sex wedding cakes. The Obama administration had not weighed in on the case, but it had taken action in legal fights to support LGBT rights. During Obama's terms, the Justice Department declined to defend a federal law that had defined marriage as between one man and one woman, and issued guidance on bathroom use by transgender students. The Obama-era Justice Department argued on behalf of legalizing same-sex marriages. "The United States has a strong interest in the eradication of discrimination on the basis of sexual orientation," the government wrote in that case, *Obergefell v. Hodges*.

The Trump administration took a different approach. The Justice Department revoked the guidance on bathroom use by transgender students. And for the first time in history, the ACLU said, the Solicitor General's Office, in the *Masterpiece Cakeshop* case, supported an exemption from an anti-discrimination law based on a constitutional right. The government's brief in the case sided with the baker who refused to bake a cake for a same-sex wedding, arguing that forcing a baker to "create expression for and participate in a ceremony that violates his sincerely held religious belief invades his First Amendment rights."

Civil rights groups criticized the government's brief as blowing a hole in anti-discrimination laws, many of which the Justice Department is supposed to enforce. The NAACP Legal Defense and Educational Fund pointed out that the case involved the invocation of religious belief as a justification for discriminatory conduct—in much the way that other cases of racial discrimination did decades ago.

One Trump administration reversal created an exceedingly rare situation in which the federal government essentially argued against itself.

The case first arrived at the Supreme Court in September 2016, just two months before Trump surprised the world by beating Hillary Clinton. Government lawyers urged the Supreme Court to hear a major workers' rights case that "affects countless employees and employers nationwide." A federal agency, the National Labor Relations Board, or NLRB, had sided with employees who wanted to band together for class-action lawsuits about overtime and other employment issues, handing a defeat to businesses that wanted to enforce arbitration clauses in work agreements. An appeals court decided the board's decision was wrong. So the Obama administration asked the Supreme Court to overturn the appeals court's ruling. A week before Trump took office, the Supreme Court agreed to hear the case that would come to be known as *Epic Systems.*

Had Clinton won the election, the federal government's pro-employee arguments almost assuredly would have stayed the same. But the new Trump administration looked at the case from a different perspective and decided the Obama-era lawyers had gotten it wrong. The Solicitor General's Office put it bluntly in a brief: "After the change in administration, the Office reconsidered the issue and has reached the opposite conclusion." The brief said NLRB and the Obama-era argument did not give "adequate weight" to one of the key issues in the case.

But in a strange twist, the Trump administration also decided that the NLRB could represent itself in the case. Lawyers from the board filed their own brief. And the case was set for oral arguments on the first day of the 2017 October Term. Acting Solicitor General Jeff Wall, arguing for the federal government, spoke for about fifteen minutes about why the NLRB was wrong. Then Richard Griffin, arguing for the federal agency, had his turn.

Almost seven months later, in a 5–4 decision that divided the court down familiar ideological lines, the Supreme Court sided with the Justice Department's approach. There's no way to know for sure whether the Trump administration's approach made the difference in the case, but that didn't stop workers' rights groups from making the connection. "Every American needs to know that the Trump administration sided not with the workers in this case, but with the corporations that want to strip away workers' rights," Christine Owens, the executive director of the National Employment Law Project, said. "As we've seen repeatedly this past year, the president's promise to put America's workers first is hollow rhetoric. This administration is eager to let corporations write the rules for the rest of us."

Ken Starr, a former solicitor general during the George H. W. Bush administration, said Francisco had "won the equivalent of the Triple Crown in horse racing" because the court sided with the Trump administration in the cases in which the solicitor general changed sides.

"Once the federal government stakes out a legal or constitutional position, the strong presumption is to keep the faith," Starr wrote in the *National Law Journal*. "But elections, like ideas, have consequences. Deeply held philosophical and policy views undergird the fashioning of specific legal positions. Those visions will naturally clash in a free society, particularly in a transition from a very progressive administration to a decidedly conservative one."

Epilogue

The Court's New Center

Ahead of the 2017 October Term, Justice Anthony Kennedy had his hands firmly on the wheel of the Supreme Court. For the previous decade before his retirement, he was almost always the justice most frequently on the prevailing side of the court's decisions. He was described as mercurial, the "sphinx of Sacramento," and the swing vote—the justice on a conservative court who gave both sides hope to prevail in major cases. At Harvard Law School in 2015, he said he hated the "swing vote" label: "The cases swing, I don't."

He might not have swung, but Kennedy steered, and the court followed.

Statistics from court-tracking site *SCOTUSblog* tell the story: Kennedy was in the majority on 98 percent and 97 percent of the court's opinions in the previous two terms. More starkly, he was in the majority more than 90 percent of the time when counting just those cases that divided the justices those terms. Compare that to less than 70 percent of the time on the winning side in at least one of those two terms for Justices Clarence Thomas, Ruth Bader Ginsburg,

Samuel A. Alito Jr., or Sonia Sotomayor. A lawyer who frequently argues before the court, Neal Katyal, told a crowd at an event previewing the 2017 October Term, "As Justice Kennedy goes, so has the court."

But in his last term, Kennedy never turned left. Democrats and their allies had hoped he would swing to their side in several cases as he had in previous terms, but he was a consistent conservative vote. After he stepped down on the last day, consensus quickly formed among lawyers, journalists, and politicians that the resulting string of 5–4 conservative rulings was a preview of the Supreme Court's future.

Who was the justice most often on the winning side during the 2017 October Term? Chief Justice John G. Roberts Jr., who rarely sides with the court's liberals in divisive cases. "I think this past term will be seen as a new era on the Supreme Court," Erwin Chemerinsky, the dean of Berkeley Law School, said at a panel discussion. "Last term there was no swing justice. From now on, I think, for years to come, decades maybe, there's not going to be a swing justice either."

The actions of the court during the 2017 October Term provide a glimpse of what the Supreme Court could look like in a post-Kennedy era: a greater chance that the court will take on more contentious issues, a greater chance the conservatives will win, and an even greater role for the chief justice in shaping the court's political moves.

Make no mistake, Kennedy was a conservative who prior to his final term on the court often sided with Republican interests in many of the court's most controversial decisions: *Bush v. Gore,* which played such a decisive role in the contested 2000 presidential election; *Citizens United v. FEC,* which allowed dark money in federal elections;

Shelby County v. Holder, which cut down a key part of the Voting Rights Act; and *D.C. v. Heller,* which established a Second Amendment right to keep a handgun in the home for protection.

But Kennedy's legacy is politically mixed because he authored landmark opinions in divisive cases that established laws that Democrats and their allies preferred: preserving access to abortion in *Planned Parenthood v. Casey;* backing same-sex marriage in *Obergefell v. Hodges;* and upholding an affirmative-action admissions plan in *Fisher v. University of Texas.* The issues on which Kennedy joined liberals are those that Senate Democrats who oppose Trump's nominee for the high court, U.S. Circuit Judge Brett Kavanaugh, say will now be at risk.

"Though the left has not been shut out, it has mostly played defense," Joshua Matz, publisher of the *Take Care* legal blog and former Kennedy clerk, wrote in an editorial in the *Washington Post.*

In the two major cases in which Democrats and their allies had held out hope for Kennedy's vote during his final term—*Gill* and *Masterpiece Cakeshop*—the conservative position won on narrow grounds, rendering it likely that the issue will return to the Supreme Court once a more reliably conservative justice is in place. "Without Justice Kennedy, I don't see a fifth vote to say that a state can force a business to serve customers even if it violates the business owner's religious beliefs. I don't see with Justice Kennedy gone, I don't see a fifth vote to find that partisan gerrymandering is unconstitutional," Erwin Chemerinsky said. "So losing Justice Kennedy in these areas, like so many, really cuts off any possibility of liberals winning for years to come."

There are other ways Kennedy influenced the court that can't be readily quantified because they are hidden in the private work of the justices. The uncertainty around how Kennedy would vote in a case might have affected the very grounds that the justices discussed and upon which they decided. "Maybe that prevented both groups from advocating for positions that were more aggressive than they would have done, knowing that they had to temper their position to potentially get Justice Kennedy's vote," Leah Litman, a former Kennedy clerk and assistant professor of law at the University of California, Irvine, said. "That's also going to disappear. The new median is now Justice Roberts."

Kennedy's uncertain positions on major issues likely also affected which cases the court agreed to take on, as highlighted in a gun-control case the justices declined to hear during the 2017 October Term. The justices discuss and vote on which cases to hear in a private conference. There are no publicly available records about those votes or the reasons for them, so trying to figure out why the court agrees to hear cases is not an exact science and is steeped in the internal politics of the court. But sometimes the justices offer clues if they write separately to discuss their thinking. The court gets thousands of appeals per year and accepts only a few dozen. It takes four affirmative votes for a case to be granted a writ of certiorari (to use the technical terminology).

The court hasn't voted to take up a gun-control case for eight years, even though there are five conservative justices. Thomas, Alito, and Gorsuch have not let the Supreme Court's inaction go unnoticed. Had those three justices voted to hear a gun-control case, and Kennedy or Roberts had joined them, that would have been enough to put the issue back on the court's docket. It never happened.

An example of this dynamic played out in February 2018. That month, a disgruntled student shot and killed seventeen students and staff at a Parkland, Florida, high school. The mass shooting would prompt nationwide marches against gun violence and renewed calls for federal legislation to ban assault-style weapons, bolster background checks for gun purchases, and more. Congress passed a law meant to more strictly enforce the current laws on background checks.

Less than a week after that shooting, the court announced it would not consider an appeal of a California law that required an average person to wait ten days after buying a gun to get it. Thomas wrote a dissent to note his objection to the court's allowing too many gun-control laws to go into effect across the nation. "The right to keep and bear arms is apparently this Court's constitutional orphan," Thomas wrote. "And the lower courts seem to have gotten the message."

That meant the court still would not weigh in on gun control since two landmark gun rights cases in 2008 and 2010. In *D.C. v. Heller,* a 5–4 decision from 2008, the court established a right to have a gun in the home for protection—but it also said the government could enact traditional and commonsense gun controls. A case in 2010 applied that ruling to the states as well. Since then, state and local governments have passed laws that ban semiautomatic rifles, limit the number of bullets a magazine can hold, clamp down on who can get a concealed-carry permit, and institute waiting periods for firearm purchases. The court had passed on every opportunity to hear challenges.

It's not readily apparent why Kennedy (or Roberts, for that matter) never provided a fourth vote to review gun cases. It's possible Kennedy doesn't see any constitutional problem with the state laws. It's possible he didn't want to have the court start wading into the legislative decisions in each state about what types of guns could be banned or what size of magazine purchased. It's possible that the other four justices didn't know how Kennedy would rule in those cases and didn't want to take a gun rights case only to have Kennedy write a decision that definitively established that states could enact these kinds of restrictions. It's even possible he did vote to take a gun-control case, but either Thomas, Alito, or Gorsuch (or Scalia, who wrote the *Heller* decision) did not vote to review it.

Trump's next appointment likely would be more willing than Kennedy to provide a fourth vote. Trump, during the campaign, said the country needed a Supreme Court that would uphold the Second Amendment, "which is under absolute siege." The views of his nominee at the time this book was written, Kavanaugh, appear to line up more with those of Thomas, Alito, and Gorsuch. In a follow-up case to *Heller,* called *Heller II,* Kavanaugh was on an appeals court panel that upheld key parts of a new D.C. ban on semiautomatic rifles and limits on the size of magazines. Kavanaugh dissented, writing that it "would strain logic and common sense" that the Second Amendment would allow semiautomatic handguns but not semiautomatic rifles, which have "not traditionally been banned and are in common use today, and are thus protected under *Heller.*"

Roberts, who also apparently hasn't provided the fourth vote to take any gun rights case, still could remain as a hurdle for the conservative judges who want to revisit the Second Amendment. It might take four votes to hear a case, but it takes five to win. The other justices might not be sure of where Roberts would want to come down, particularly because of his role in guiding the institution.

Roberts could choose which side wins and assign himself to author the opinion, said Lawrence Friedman, a professor of constitutional law at New England Law in Boston. And Roberts would have to weigh whether to spend the court's institutional capital on gun cases. This underscores just how much control Roberts will have on the court going forward. "With four presumably reliable conservative votes, he'll be in a unique position to decide where, how far, and how fast, the court goes," Gregory G. Garre, a solicitor general during the George W. Bush administration, told the *Washington Post*. "This will put the chief in more of a swing justice role, and make him one of the most powerful chief justices in recent history."

The court's *Roe v. Wade* decision will be threatened with a Trump pick on the court. Trump's campaign promise was to appoint justices who oppose *Roe*. From the liberal perspective, the question is whether his second appointment will help the Republican Party overturn the case entirely—which has been an animating political goal on the right for decades—or simply diminish access to abortion by allowing states to pass and enforce stricter abortion laws. An appeals court decision in July 2018 that struck down an eighteen-hour waiting period after an ultrasound before allowing an abortion might be the perfect case to clarify the matter.

There are other numerous cases in the pipeline that could test the court. There's an Obamacare case in Texas. There are numerous cases dealing with the unusual strains

Trump is putting on the country, with lawsuits about his immigration policies, the intermingling of his business dealings and White House business, the possibility of the special counsel probe subpoenaing him or charging him with a crime, and more.

The justices are nine people, and any group of nine people will be influenced by a new member. At the beginning of the term, the discussion was about Gorsuch. Katyal cautioned that it's always hard to determine a justice's approach so soon in a job that has lifetime tenure, such as the trajectory of Chief Justice John G. Roberts Jr. after his 2005 appointment. Court watchers said Roberts was in lockstep with the conservative wing, but then he voted to save the 2010 health care law.

As Garre told a panel before the 2017 October Term, the court sometimes behaves in "weird ways" when a new justice enters the mix. His example was when President George H. W. Bush appointed the conservative Thomas to the court in 1991. Everyone thought the court that included Justice Sandra Day O'Connor, another Ronald Reagan pick, would become much more conservative when Thomas joined, Garre said. "But strangely enough, what he did is push Justice O'Connor to the left," Garre said. He was talking about Gorsuch, but it applies just as much to the next justice, who is expected to be confirmed later this year, after this book is published.

From outside the building, where protestors line the sidewalk on the days that big decisions are released, the Supreme Court will remain embroiled in the political and cultural turbulence that is rocking the nation. Inside the building, the court will continue shifting for years to come.

Appendix

Biographies of Current Justices of the Supreme Court

All biographies are derived from the U.S. Supreme Court website https://www.supremecourt.gov/about/biographies.aspx.

Chief Justice

John G. Roberts Jr., chief justice of the United States, was born in Buffalo, New York, on January 27, 1955. He married Jane Marie Sullivan in 1996, and they have two children—Josephine and Jack. He received an AB from Harvard College in 1976 and a JD from Harvard Law School in 1979. He served as a law clerk for Judge Henry J. Friendly of the U.S. Court of Appeals for the Second Circuit from 1979 to 1980 and as a law clerk for then Associate Justice William H. Rehnquist of the Supreme Court of the United States during the 1980 term. He was special assistant to the attorney general, U.S. Department of Justice from 1981 to 1982; associate counsel to President Ronald Reagan, White House Counsel's Office from 1982 to 1986; and principal deputy solicitor general, U.S.

127

Department of Justice from 1989 to 1993. From 1986 to 1989 and 1993 to 2003, he practiced law in Washington, D.C. He was appointed to the U.S. Court of Appeals for the District of Columbia Circuit in 2003. President George W. Bush nominated him as chief justice of the United States, and he took his seat on September 29, 2005.

Associate Justices

Justices are listed in descending order of seniority.

Clarence Thomas was born in the Pinpoint community near Savannah, Georgia, on June 23, 1948. He attended Conception Seminary from 1967 to 1968 and received an AB, cum laude, from Holy Cross College in 1971 and a JD from Yale Law School in 1974. He was admitted to law practice in Missouri in 1974 and served as an assistant attorney general of Missouri, 1974–1977; as an attorney with the Monsanto Company, 1977–1979; and as a legislative assistant to Senator John Danforth, 1979–1981. From 1981 to 1982, he served as assistant secretary for civil rights in the U.S. Department of Education, and he served as chairman of the U.S. Equal Employment Opportunity Commission from 1982 to 1990. From 1990 to 1991, he served as a judge on the U.S. Court of Appeals for the District of Columbia Circuit. President George H. W. Bush nominated him as an associate justice of the Supreme Court, and he took his seat on October 23, 1991. He married Virginia Lamp on May 30, 1987, and has one child, Jamal Adeen, by a previous marriage.

Ruth Bader Ginsburg was born in Brooklyn, New York, on March 15, 1933. She married Martin D. Ginsburg in 1954 and has a daughter, Jane, and a son, James. She received her BA from Cornell University, attended Harvard Law School, and received her LLB from Columbia Law School. She served as a law clerk to the Honorable Edmund L. Palmieri, judge of the U.S. District Court for the Southern District of New York, from 1959 to 1961. From 1961 to 1963, she was a research associate and then associate director of the Columbia Law School Project on International Procedure. She was a professor of law at Rutgers University School of Law from 1963 to 1972 and Columbia Law School from 1972 to 1980 and served as a fellow at the Center for Advanced Study in the Behavioral Sciences in Stanford, California, from 1977 to 1978. In 1971, she was instrumental in launching the Women's Rights Project of the American Civil Liberties Union and served as the ACLU's general counsel from 1973 to 1980 and on the National Board of Directors from 1974 to 1980. She was appointed a judge of the U.S. Court of Appeals for the District of Columbia Circuit in 1980. President Bill Clinton nominated her as an associate justice of the Supreme Court, and she took her seat on August 10, 1993.

Stephen G. Breyer was born in San Francisco, California, on August 15, 1938. He married Joanna Hare in 1967 and has three children—Chloe, Nell, and Michael. He received an AB from Stanford University, a BA from Magdalen College, Oxford, and an LLB from Harvard Law School. He served as a law clerk to Justice Arthur

Goldberg of the Supreme Court of the United States during the 1964 term; as a special assistant to the assistant U.S. attorney general for antitrust, 1965–1967; as an assistant special prosecutor of the Watergate Special Prosecution Force, 1973; as special counsel of the U.S. Senate Judiciary Committee, 1974–1975; and as chief counsel of the committee, 1979–1980. He was an assistant professor, professor of law, and lecturer at Harvard Law School, 1967–1994; a professor at the Harvard University Kennedy School of Government, 1977–1980; and a visiting professor at the College of Law, Sydney, Australia, and at the University of Rome. From 1980 to 1990, he served as a judge of the U.S. Court of Appeals for the First Circuit, and he continued as its chief judge, 1990–1994. He also served as a member of the Judicial Conference of the United States, 1990–1994, and on the U.S. Sentencing Commission, 1985–1989. President Clinton nominated him as an associate justice of the Supreme Court, and he took his seat on August 3, 1994.

Samuel A. Alito Jr. was born in Trenton, New Jersey, on April 1, 1950. He married Martha-Ann Bomgardner in 1985 and has two children—Philip and Laura. He served as a law clerk for Leonard I. Garth of the U.S. Court of Appeals for the Third Circuit from 1976 to 1977. He was assistant U.S. attorney, District of New Jersey, 1977–1981; assistant to the solicitor general, U.S. Department of Justice, 1981–1985; deputy assistant attorney general, U.S. Department of Justice, 1985–1987; and U.S. attorney, District of New Jersey, 1987–1990. He was appointed to the U.S. Court of Appeals for the Third Circuit in 1990.

President George W. Bush nominated him as an associate justice of the Supreme Court, and he took his seat on January 31, 2006.

Sonia Sotomayor was born in Bronx, New York, on June 25, 1954. She earned a BA in 1976 from Princeton University, graduating summa cum laude and receiving the university's highest academic honor. In 1979, she earned a JD from Yale Law School, where she served as an editor of the *Yale Law Journal*. She served as assistant district attorney in the New York County District Attorney's Office from 1979 to 1984. She then litigated international commercial matters in New York City at Pavia and Harcourt, where she served as an associate and then partner from 1984 to 1992. In 1991, President George H. W. Bush nominated her to the U.S. District Court, Southern District of New York, and she served in that role from 1992 to 1998. She served as a judge on the U.S. Court of Appeals for the Second Circuit from 1998 to 2009. President Barack Obama nominated her as an associate justice of the Supreme Court on May 26, 2009, and she assumed this role on August 8, 2009.

Elena Kagan was born in New York, New York, on April 28, 1960. She received an AB from Princeton in 1981, an MPhil from Oxford in 1983, and a JD from Harvard Law School in 1986. She clerked for Judge Abner Mikva of the U.S. Court of Appeals for the District of Columbia Circuit from 1986 to 1987 and for Justice Thurgood Marshall of the U.S. Supreme Court during the 1987 term. After briefly practicing law at a Washington, D.C. law firm, she became a law professor, first at the University of Chicago Law School and later at Harvard Law School. She also served for four years in the Clinton administration as associate counsel to the president and then as deputy assistant to the president for domestic policy. Between 2003 and 2009, she served as the dean of Harvard Law School. In 2009, President Obama nominated her as the solicitor general of the United States. A year later, the president nominated her as an associate justice of the Supreme Court on May 10, 2010. She took her seat on August 7, 2010.

Neil M. Gorsuch was born in Denver, Colorado, on August 29, 1967. He and his wife, Louise, have two daughters. He received a BA from Columbia University, a JD from Harvard Law School, and a DPhil from Oxford University. He served as a law clerk to Judge David B. Sentelle of the U.S. Court of Appeals for the District of Columbia Circuit and as a law clerk to Justice Byron White and Justice Anthony M. Kennedy of the Supreme Court of the United States. From 1995 to 2005, he was in private practice, and from 2005 to 2006, he was principal deputy associate attorney general at the U.S. Department of Justice. He was appointed to the U.S. Court of Appeals for the Tenth Circuit in 2006. He served on the Standing Committee on Rules for Practice and Procedure of the U.S. Judicial Conference and as chairman of the Advisory Committee on Rules of Appellate Procedure. He taught at the University of Colorado Law School. President Donald J. Trump nominated him as an associate justice of the Supreme Court, and he took his seat on April 10, 2017.

Retired Justices

All justices are listed in order of retirement.

Sandra Day O'Connor, associate justice, was born in El Paso, Texas, on March 26, 1930. She married John Jay O'Connor III in 1952 and has three sons—Scott, Brian, and Jay. She received her BA and LLB from Stanford University. She served as deputy county attorney of San Mateo County, California, from 1952 to 1953 and as a civilian attorney for the Quartermaster Market Center, Frankfurt, Germany, from 1954 to 1957. From 1958 to 1960, she practiced law in Maryvale, Arizona, and served as assistant attorney general of Arizona from 1965 to 1969. She was appointed to the Arizona State Senate in 1969 and was subsequently reelected twice for two-year terms. In 1975, she was elected judge of the Maricopa County Superior Court and served until 1979, when she was appointed to the Arizona Court of Appeals. President Reagan nominated her as an associate justice of the Supreme Court, and she took her seat on September 25, 1981. Justice O'Connor retired from the Supreme Court on January 31, 2006.

David H. Souter, associate justice, was born in Melrose, Massachusetts, on September 17, 1939. He graduated from Harvard College, from which he received his AB. After two years as a Rhodes Scholar at Magdalen College, Oxford, he received an AB in jurisprudence from Oxford University and an MA in 1989. After receiving an LLB from Harvard Law School, he was an associate at Orr and Reno in Concord, New Hampshire, from 1966 to 1968, when he became an assistant attorney general of New Hampshire. In 1971, he became deputy attorney general and, in 1976, attorney general of New Hampshire. In 1978, he was named an associate justice of the Superior Court of New Hampshire and was appointed to the Supreme Court of New Hampshire as an associate justice in 1983. He became a judge of the U.S. Court of Appeals for the First Circuit on May 25, 1990. President George H. W. Bush nominated him as an associate justice of the Supreme Court, and he took his seat on October 9, 1990. Justice Souter retired from the Supreme Court on June 29, 2009.

John Paul Stevens, associate justice, was born in Chicago, Illinois, on April 20, 1920. He married Maryan Mulholland (deceased) and has four children—John Joseph, Kathryn, Elizabeth Jane, and Susan Roberta. He received an AB from the University of Chicago and a JD from Northwestern University School of Law. He served in the U.S. Navy from 1942 to 1945 and was a law clerk to Justice Wiley Rutledge of the Supreme Court of the United States during the 1947 term. He was admitted to law practice in Illinois in 1949. He was associate counsel to the Subcommittee on the Study of Monopoly Power of the Judiciary Committee of the U.S. House of Representatives, 1951–1952, and a member of the attorney general's National Committee to Study Antitrust Law, 1953–1955. He was second vice president of the Chicago Bar Association in 1970. From 1970 to 1975, he served as a judge of the U.S. Court of Appeals for the Seventh Circuit. President Gerald Ford nominated him as an associate justice of the Supreme Court, and he took his seat on December 19, 1975. Justice Stevens retired from the Supreme Court on June 29, 2010.

Anthony M. Kennedy was born in Sacramento, California, on July 23, 1936. He married Mary Davis and has three children. He received his BA from Stanford University and the London School of Economics and his LLB from Harvard Law School. He was in private practice in San Francisco, California, from 1961 to 1963, as well as in Sacramento, California, from 1963 to 1975. From 1965 to 1988, he was a professor of constitutional law at the McGeorge School of Law, University of the Pacific. He has served in numerous positions during his career, including as a member of the California Army National Guard in 1961, on the board of the Federal Judicial Center from 1987 to 1988, and on two committees of the Judicial Conference of the United States: the Advisory Panel on Financial Disclosure Reports and Judicial Activities (subsequently renamed the Advisory Committee on Codes of Conduct) from 1979 to 1987 and the Committee on Pacific Territories from 1979 to 1990, which he chaired from 1982 to 1990. He was appointed to the U.S. Court of Appeals for the Ninth Circuit in 1975. President Reagan nominated him as an associate justice of the Supreme Court, and he took his seat on February 18, 1988. Justice Kennedy retired from the Supreme Court on July 31, 2018.

Acknowledgments

This book came together at the speed of journalism and was not a solo effort. Damon Linker, my editor, provided deft edits and well-timed doses of encouragement. Reassurance from a knowledgeable guide was invaluable when a deadline fast approached. It was an honor to have Garrett Epps suggest me as an author for this series and talk me through an approach to the task. I always learn something from a conversation with Garrett, whether in the Supreme Court press room or killing time in the courtroom's cramped alcoves as we wait for the justices to take their seats. To Damon and Garrett, thank you so much.

I glean information from chats with the many skilled and collegial journalists who cover the justices. Kimberly Robinson went above and beyond in sharing the wisdom she gained from writing last year's entry in this series. Kimberly's knowledge of the cases of each term is hard to beat, and her reading of chapter drafts put my mind at ease. Similarly, John Gramlich, who previously reported on the Supreme Court, proved he was a generous friend with great insights about my work. Thanks to you both, and a hearty five-minute buzzer salute.

Acknowledgments

CQ Roll Call has given me an opportunity to tackle the greatest news beat, the Supreme Court and the country's legal system, from the perspective of Congress and politics. The work I do there informed this book to a great degree. The late Steve Komarow, *CQ*'s top editor at the time, gave me the official approval for this project without running the decision further up corporate channels. Because, he said, "life's too short." Michael Scarcella opened the door for me to report on the law in Washington, D.C. at the *National Law Journal*. Cheers, guys.

The *SCOTUSblog* site made research much faster and is truly a great resource, especially the annual stat pack that makes it easier to identify broader trends. There are numerous law professors, lawyers, and judges who make up the vibrant dialogue that surrounds everything courts do, who notice every detail, who pick up on the slightest nuance, and who share those views. I have benefited from their expertise throughout my career covering the courts. From local courts to the Supreme Court, it's been a joy to learn. I appreciate all of it.

Most important, my parents, John and Jean, raised me in a home full of unconditional love and encouragement. They gave me all I needed to pursue whatever I wanted to do. It means everything.